Dictation Resource Book

Susan C. Anthony

Instructional Resources Company
P.O. Box 111704
Anchorage, Alaska 99511-1704
www.SusanCAnthony.com

Teach with less effort, more SUCCESS!

Instructional Resources Company aims to assist teachers in maintaining high objective standards while helping *all* students reach them. Our materials and workshops are designed to save teachers time while helping them nurture the excitement of learning in their students, build confidence through early success, and build a framework of background information to which new learning can be connected throughout life. We welcome feedback from anyone using our materials.

Instructional Resources Company
P.O. Box 111704
Anchorage, AK 99511-1704
(907) 345-6689

Instructional Resources Company
3235 Garland
Wheat Ridge, CO 80033
Susan@SusanCAnthony.com

*Check the web site, **www.SusanCAnthony.com**, for information on Susan's books and workshops, including free sample activities to try out with students. Some of Susan's books include:*

Spelling	*Spelling Plus: 1000 Words toward Spelling Success* *Dictation Resource Book for use with Spelling Plus* *Homophones Resource Book*
Reference	*Facts Plus: An Almanac of Essential Information* *Facts Plus Activity Book*
Mathematics	*Addition Facts in Five Minutes a Day* *Subtraction Facts in Five Minutes a Day* *Multiplication Facts in Five Minutes a Day* *Division Facts in Five Minutes a Day* *Casting Nines: A Quick Check for Math Computation*
Writing	*Poetry from the Heart* *Manuscript Handwriting Masters* *Cursive Handwriting Masters*

Note: Although the author and publisher have exhaustively researched all sources to ensure the accuracy of the information contained in this book, we assume no responsibility for errors, inaccuracies, omissions or any other inconsistency herein. Any slights against people or organizations are unintentional.

ISBN 1-879478-21-8

CONTENTS

Why Dictation? 1

Setting Standards for Written Work 3

Dictation Step by Step 7
    Spelling Plus 1000 Word Core List 9
    Lists by Level 11
    Checklist of Language Objectives 13
    Dictation Planning Worksheet 16

Dictation Sentences 17
    Letter Form 36
    Bibliographic and Outline Form 38

Capitalization 39
    Abbreviations 52

Punctuation 53

Prefixes and Suffixes 55

Grammar and Parts of Speech 63

Word Histories 77

TIPS FOR SURVEYING THE *DICTATION RESOURCE BOOK*

- Although there are parts of the *Dictation Resource Book* that could be of value to any teacher, it is specifically designed to accompany the *Spelling Plus* program, also available from Instructional Resources Company. The purpose of this book is to save teachers time as they use sentence dictation to review the 1000 core words in *Spelling Plus* while teaching specific language concepts and skills. The 1000 core words are listed alphabetically on pp. 9–10.

- Scan pp. 1–2 for the rationale for using sentence dictation. Especially notice the creative/critical "bridge" on p. 2. Dictation is an important, even essential, part of this bridge.

- See pp. 7–8 for step-by-step directions. They will help you to see how dictation might fit into your own teaching situation.

- Scan pp. 13–15 for a list of specific objectives that can be taught during dictation. Although planning time is required to prepare appropriate and challenging sentences that address the needs of your unique students, it would take time to teach these objectives in other ways as well. Dictation is an effective and efficient use of instructional time because it can be used to teach and review numerous objectives in just 10–15 minutes a day.

- The sentences on pp. 18–35 are a "starter set", which will allow you to try dictation with a minimum investment of time so that you can see for yourself how effective it can be. Do not expect immediate improvement in students' personal writing. In my experience, progress is slow at first but invariably gains momentum. Within a few months, there is *amazing* improvement. Additional sentences may be found in the Resources section of the web site: www.SusanCAnthony.com. The best sentences will be those you write yourself to match your students' specific needs.

WHY DICTATION?

Teachers know that few if any students will show improvement in their own writing as a result of isolated instruction in spelling, capitalization, or punctuation. Dictation is the single most effective strategy I've found for teaching and reviewing to *mastery* almost anything covered in a typical language text with the exception of creative writing. It is an essential link between *instruction* in spelling and mechanics and *application* in real writing. It is also a very efficient use of time. It takes only about 10 minutes to dictate and have students write, check and correct four sentences a day. With dictation and the writing process, I can teach almost anything in the language curriculum so that by the end of the year, students *apply* the skills as they write.

As adults fluent in writing, we often forget how much one must know and apply in order to correctly write a "simple" sentence:
— Capitalize the first word.
— Recognize and capitalize all proper nouns.
— Remember spellings of any words needed. For example, a child must recall whether to spell a word with the sound as it's spelled in *came, day, they, wait, great, eight, straight, veil,* or even *gauge.*
— Recognize when a word needs an ending and when it's a base word: *tax / tacks.*
— Remember and apply rules for adding endings: *hop + ed = hopped, hope + ed = hoped, city + es = cities, lone + ly = lonely.* Remember irregular cases such as *truly.*
— Recognize whether a word is a homophone and choose the correct spelling.
— Recognize whether a word is a contraction or possessive needing an apostrophe.
— Recognize when a comma is needed and place it correctly.
— Determine the type of sentence and ending punctuation.

All this is necessary to write a single sentence. In real writing, there are also paragraphs, form, and dialogue. It would be virtually impossible for learners to remember all of this while their minds are engaged in creative thinking and writing. It is unrealistic for teachers to expect that they will. Creative thinking is incompatible with the critical thinking needed to remember spelling and mechanics. Even as adults, we generally function better when we creatively and freely brainstorm solutions to a problem, then go back to critically consider each possible solution. Literate adults are able to write creatively and correctly at the same time because they have *mastered* basic spelling and the mechanics of writing to the point that they require almost no conscious thought.

As teachers, we must realize that most children need our assistance in bridging the gap between the creative and critical aspects of writing. I teach the writing process concurrently with spelling and mechanics, but separately. At the same time, I build a bridge from critical toward creative with dictation, and from creative toward critical with personal words and editing. Improved first draft writing is the goal.

ADVANTAGES OF DICTATION

— Dictation provides a means for extended and mixed review of spellings, especially of homophones. Although daily practice and homework ensure that correct spellings are *stored* in memory, dictation provides the repetition and day-after-day review needed to practice *recalling* spellings when needed in the course of writing. Without such practice, it is unlikely that spelling in writing will markedly improve.
— Students are not asked to think creatively and critically at the same time during

dictation. Sentences are supplied by the teacher so the students can focus on form.

— Dictation is routine. The process is basically the same every day—familiar, secure, and comfortable. Students' minds are free to concentrate on concepts rather than directions.

— Dictation provides a means of introducing capitalization and punctuation rules one element at a time, focusing on the new element intensively for a while, then gradually tapering off the amount of practice as students achieve mastery. Periodic review can continue indefinitely.

— Students learn to carefully check and correct their own work. Self-correction is positively correlated with learning.

— Dictation proceeds from oral language to written language. Some methods for teaching checking and correcting give students sentences containing deliberate mistakes and ask them to find and correct the mistakes. I avoid this approach until students are *quite* good at spelling. There's always a risk that one child's mind will "snap a picture" of an incorrect spelling, and *that* will be the impression that remains. With dictation, the only mistakes children see and correct are their own.

— Students receive immediate objective feedback. They correct any errors they find without penalty or teacher intervention.

— Teachers can be flexible with dictation, introducing new concepts as soon as they feel confident that their particular students are ready and not before.

— Teachers can lift dictation sentences directly from student writing or use the names of their own students in sentences to reinforce the connection between dictation and writing.

— The 10-15 minutes a day of dictation result in more long-term benefits than I've seen with any other use of that time.

— The dictation paper collected from each child at the end of a week provides me with up to three grades: spelling, language and handwriting.

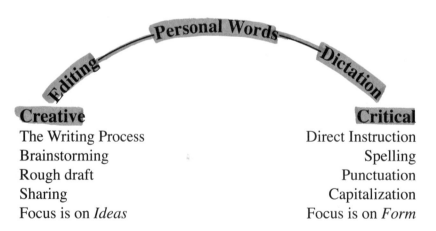

Creative
The Writing Process
Brainstorming
Rough draft
Sharing
Focus is on *Ideas*

Critical
Direct Instruction
Spelling
Punctuation
Capitalization
Focus is on *Form*

The goal is in dictation is eventual synthesis between the creative and critical aspects of writing. It *is* possible for children to learn to write creatively and correctly at the same time. Literate adults can do it. Both creativity and correctness are important, and balance between the two is possible. If a person has no ideas to communicate, excellence in spelling and mechanics is useless. On the other hand, if a person has a great deal to communicate but cannot do so in standard written English, he or she is operating with a handicap. His/her ideas are unlikely to receive the serious consideration they may deserve.

SETTING STANDARDS FOR WRITTEN WORK

For the first several years I taught, my spirits would fall as I read through the first student writing samples in September. I was just getting acquainted with the class and didn't want to be negative or punitive, but how could I honestly say their work was acceptable when it wasn't? I felt I would set a bad precedent by accepting substandard work.

I tried a number of approaches to this problem before finding an effective way to set high standards early in the year while helping students earn and experience true success. I've used this with fourth to sixth graders. Adapt it as you like.

Starting the second day of school, I teach students how to head their papers and the form I want them to use for questions and answers. They each need a pencil and a piece of notebook paper, plus a set of "who" questions (p. 5).

— Get a piece of notebook paper from your folder or binder. *No ripped paper will be accepted.*

— Turn the paper so the front side is up. The holes should be on the left, so that when the page is in a binder, you'll see the front side of the page first.

— Use pencil. With ink, if there's a mistake, you'll have to start over from the beginning. With pencil, you can erase small mistakes gently and carefully.

— Write the title, *"Who" Questions,* on the top line, centered and capitalized.

— Use your best handwriting. This should be an example of the best work you can do.

— Skip a line. Do not write anything on the second line.

— Write your first and last name on the third line, beginning at the red margin. Last names are very important in junior high.

— Write the date on the same line, beginning about two and a half inches from the right edge of the paper. Month date comma year: *January 25, 2008.*

— Skip a line. Do not write anything on the fourth line.

— Write **1.** on the outside of the red margin line on the fifth line.

— Copy the first question *exactly,* beginning at the red margin line. Start with a capital letter and end with a question mark. If you come to the red margin line that shows through from the other side before you come to the end of the sentence, finish the word you're writing and write the next word on the next line, starting at the red margin line. Do not squeeze words on the line. Do not divide words. If a word is too long to fit on a line, put the entire word on the next line.

— Check each word, letter for letter, to be sure you copied correctly.

— After you've written and checked the question, go to the next line and write the answer in a complete sentence. Eventually, when you have learned how to answer questions with complete sentences that contain the information in the question, there will be no need to copy questions. The answers to "who" questions should be identical to the questions, except substitute the answer in place of the word "who" and use a period at the end. For example:
Who invented chewing gum?
Charles Adams invented chewing gum.

— Check each word, letter for letter, to be sure you copied correctly. Make sure you have correct capitalization and a period at the end.

— Skip a line.

— Write **2.** on the outside of the red margin line on the next line, and continue. Do as much as you can in the time allowed (about an hour).

I tell students not to worry if they don't finish. I'm more interested in seeing their best work than in having everything done quickly. We'll practice with different kinds of questions until they can do this easily.

I circulate around the room to answer questions and help individuals. At the end of the allotted time, I collect the papers. I grade these according to my true standards, circling mistakes in red and giving a lot of F's and D's.

The next day, before returning the papers, I make these remarks: "It takes some time to adjust to being back in school after being free all summer! You haven't had to think much about writing since last May. I understand. It's normal that it will take awhile to get into the swing of things, for teachers as well as students!

"I graded the papers you did yesterday and I wasn't surprised that they weren't too good. It's been a long time since you've done anything like this, and there were a *lot* of directions to follow! I'm going to hand these back so that you can look at them, but don't worry. These grades aren't going into the grade book, and your parents will not see them. They'll just see the *best* paper you do after you've practiced. After you've looked at your papers, I'll collect them we can just throw them away."

I do this, and then introduce a new set of questions, "what" questions, reviewing the directions from yesterday, with a focus on common mistakes I saw. These papers are usually much better, in the C and D range. I focus specifically on improvements I see, then introduce "when" questions, teaching them how to choose between the preposition *in* (*in* July or *in* 1990), and *on* (*on* Monday or *on* July 2).

Before long, a few students turn in perfect papers. I congratulate these students and encourage everyone else to keep trying, they're getting closer to excellence every day! I don't record a grade until I have a student's best work. As soon as a student turns in an A+ paper, I contact the parents, record the grade, and post the paper on the wall. Once a child has earned an A+, he/she can stop copying questions and write just the answers, in complete sentences. The time saved can be used for reading, doing challenge activities, or coaching others.

Every day the grades improve, until within a week or so, all or nearly all children have A's or B's. If some can't finish all ten questions because they write slowly or have some other special difficulty, I make allowances to let them complete papers at home, or grade more on quality than quantity. The goal is for each child to complete *one* perfect paper. Not everyone reaches that goal, but most come close. The best paper a child does is the only one that counts. The rest go into the trash.

I give students lots of congratulations for excellent papers. When most of them have super papers, I invite the principal in to see what they've done and to express pride and pleasure. Students who had the most difficulty reaching the goal receive special praise for persisting despite discouragement and frustration, for believing in themselves and not giving up because of temporary setbacks. Success in life is generally not easy or automatic. What counts more than *anything* is persistence!

This activity is an excellent lead-up to dictation, where students must focus on specific details of writing, and carefully check and correct their work. I found that the neatness and quality of papers throughout the year remained acceptable when I started with this activity. Students felt justly proud of themselves and worked hard to experience again the wonderful feeling of success.

"Who" Questions

1. Who invented chewing gum?	Charles Adams
2. Who delivered the Gettysburg Address?	Abraham Lincoln
3. Who conquered the Incas in Peru?	Pizarro
4. Who discovered X rays?	Roentgen
5. Who was the first man in space?	Yuri Gagarin
6. Who was the seventh president of the United States?	Andrew Jackson
7. Who wrote the Star-Spangled Banner?	Francis Scott Key
8. Who won the first Super Bowl?	Green Bay
9. Who developed the idea of the atom?	Democritus
10. Who wrote the first dictionary?	Samuel Johnson

"What" Questions

1. What is the most famous volcano in Indonesia?	Krakatau
2. What is the capital of Peru?	Lima
3. What are the most distant objects in the universe?	quasars
4. What is another name for Vitamin C?	ascorbic acid
5. What is the German word for Friday?	Freitag
6. What is the language in Austria?	German
7. What is another name for Memorial Day?	Decoration Day
8. What is the largest island in the world?	Greenland
9. What was the original name for the month of July?	Quintilis
10. What is the highest mountain in Africa?	Kilimanjaro

"When" Questions

1. When was the U.S. motto adopted?	July 30, 1956
2. When was Martin Luther King, Jr. shot?	1968
3. When was Halley's Comet last seen?	1986
4. When was the big San Francisco earthquake?	April 18, 1906
5. When was the California gold rush?	1849
6. When was President John Kennedy born?	May 29, 1917
7. When is Flag Day?	June 14
8. When was the United States divided into time zones?	1883
9. When was the Declaration of Independence signed?	July 4, 1776
10. When was the elevator invented?	1854

More "When" Questions

1. When did Texas enter the Union?   December 29, 1845
2. When did the space shuttle Challenger explode?   January 28, 1986
3. When did Karl Marx die?   1883
4. When did Robbert Goddard invent the rocket?   1926
5. When did Sputnik I orbit the earth?   October 4, 1956
6. When did Mesa Verde become a National Park?   June 29, 1906
7. When did Mt. St. Helens erupt?   May 18, 1980
8. When did Magellan's ship circle the globe?   1522
9. When did the planet Neptune cross outside Pluto's orbit?   January 23, 1979
10. When was Martin Luther King born?   January 15, 1929

"Where" Questions

1. Where is Paris?   France
2. Where is Redwood National Park?   California
3. Where is Spain?   Europe
4. Where was George Washington born?   Virginia
5. Where is Lake Chad?   Africa
6. Where is the Liberty Bell?   Philadelphia
7. Where is the Black Sea?   Asia
8. Where was the bicycle invented?   France
9. Where are the pyramids?   Egypt
10. Where is Iraq?   the Middle East

Questions

1. Who was the tenth president?   John Tyler
2. What is the capital of Nepal?   Kathmandu
3. When was the zipper invented?   1893
4. Where was the first Thanksgiving?   Plymouth Colony
5. What ended after the Civil War?   slavery
6. Who wrote Peter Pan?   James Barrie
7. When was Voyager 1 launched?   August 20, 1977
8. Where is Mt. Cook?   New Zealand
9. When was the Bill of Rights ratified?   December 15, 1791
10. What did Stephen Foster write?   songs

DICTATION STEP BY STEP

WRITING THE SENTENCES

▪ Have a copy of the 1000 word list from *Spelling Plus* available for easy reference (pp. 9–12). Include *all* words from last week's spelling list in this week's dictation, as well as any words from previous spelling lists, especially those that continue to be misspelled in student writing. Copy the list anew each year if you wish, and highlight words as you teach them in spelling.

▪ Be aware of what homophones and language skills you've taught so that you can write sentences to review them. Use one of these two alternatives for keeping track of what you've taught, or use your own system:
  1. Checklist of objectives (pp. 13–15). Check off those you teach or review.
  2. Chronological list of objectives. List objectives as you teach them. Review recently taught skills intensively, and continue to periodically review and reteach *all* objectives.

▪ Choose one or more specific objectives to emphasize during the week (preferably one). Base your decision on what fits with the previous week's spelling list, what your students need in own their writing, or your own preferences. In general, move from more important objectives to less important ones. End-of-sentence punctuation, for example, is *far* more important than the use of hyphens. Give students plenty of time to *master* an objective before introducing another one that might be confusing. Dictate apostrophes in contractions for *months* before introducing apostrophes in possessives, or you may begin to see apostrophes on every word ending with an *s*! The planning form on p. 16 may be helpful as you write your sentences.

▪ You may use pp. 18–35 or the *Homophones Resource Book* as a source of ideas or sentences, or take sentences directly from student writing. Use the names of your own students in sentences when possible.

▪ If you are dictating to students in more than one grade level, try writing just one set of sentences. In the first two sentences, use words everyone should know. For the third sentence, use words from the middle level. The last sentence can be at the level of the most advanced student. Younger children may attempt the more difficult sentences. They will have a chance to check and correct anything they missed. Homophones, capitalization and punctuation rules, etc. can be taught to all levels at the same time. Audiotapes and mp3 recordings are available by special request for *Spelling Plus* levels C-G if your students are at widely different levels.

▪ Once sentences have been written, prepare any materials you will need to introduce the new language skill or homophone.

▪ Reserve 15–20 minutes a day for the dictation activity, depending on the amount of language instruction.

Notes

_____

_____

_____

_____

_____

_____

_____

_____

_____

DICTATING THE SENTENCES

- On Mondays, students get out a fresh sheet of notebook paper and head it. Tell them in advance whether you will dictate numbered sentences, paragraphs, a letter, or something else so they will use the correct form.

- Dictate each sentence, using the following directives. The teacher's words are bold.
  The sentence is: *What's the difference?*
  Say: *What's the difference?*
  Students say the sentence quietly aloud.
  Write: *What's the difference?*
  Students write the sentence. Teacher
  circulates around the room,
  complimenting individuals on neatness,
  remembering correct spellings,
  homophones, capitalization, etc. Focus
  on reinforcing progress for specific
  individuals when possible. Repeat the
  sentence softly if it's long, but work
  toward improving auditory memory. As
  students finish, move toward the front of
  the room.
  **Is there anything special you need
  to remember in that sentence?**
  Apostrophe in *what's,* question mark,
  difference spelled with *-ence*.
  **How many people remembered the
  apostrophe?** (etc.) **Good job! If you
  didn't, change yours now.**
  Teacher writes the sentence on the board,
  saying each letter, punctuation mark, etc.
  aloud: **Capital w - h - a - t - apostrophe
  - s** *What's* **t - h - e** *the* **d - i - f - f - e - r
  - e - n - c - e** *difference* **question mark.**
  Check and correct your sentence.
  Students check and correct.

- On Tuesdays through Fridays, students write their sentences on the same piece of paper they began Monday. The only exception is letter writing, when they use a new piece of paper each day. This paper is folded (correctly) and addressed like an envelope.

GRADING THE SENTENCES

- After Friday's dictation, students turn in their papers with all of the week's sentences. If they were absent one or more of the days, they should write "absent Tuesday" on the paper so they don't lose credit for the missing sentences. I don't have them make these up. Although it's best to dictate every day of the week, some years I've only dictated on Mondays to Thursdays because of extreme time pressure.

- Students must turn in all sentences dictated unless they were absent. To prevent the loss of papers during the week, I have students store them in special colored folders in their desks. Dictation papers may not be taken home until they've been graded. If a paper is lost, the student must head a new piece of paper and will lose credit for the missing sentences. If a lost paper is found before it's due, it may be turned in without penalty.

- I check the papers, circling every mistake. I award three grades for dictation:
  1. Handwriting: based on neatness and correct formation of letters.
  2. Spelling: I deduct five percentage points from 100% for each error.
  3. Language: I deduct five percentage points from 100% for each capitalization, punctuation, form or homophone error.

What about students who work slowly?
This is a group activity and there is pressure on students who work slowly. Otherwise, the faster students would be bored. I gauge when to move on by noticing when *most* students are ready. Slower students may continue to write as the group begins checking and discussing anything special about the sentence. They check from the sentence on the board when they're ready.

1000 Word Core Spelling List

Number indicates the list on which the word is introduced in Spelling Plus

4 a	4 and	41 because	45 busy
52 a lot	28 animal	24 become	7 but
54 able	25 another	15 been	40 buy
17 about	53 answer	41 before	10 by
14 above	21 any	29 began	58 calendar
57 absent	37 anybody	29 begin	9 call
59 accept	37 anyway	35 beginning	19 called
63 accident	67 apologize	19 being	11 came
63 accidentally	67 apology	33 believe	4 can
65 accommodate	65 appear	31 below	22 can't
54 ache	67 appearance	61 benefit	25 cannot
66 achieve	69 appreciate	5 best	49 captain
67 acquaint	65 approach	34 better	16 car
67 acquaintance	52 April	41 between	28 care
46 across	55 arctic	57 bicycle	38 careful
24 act	6 are	6 big	60 carefully
58 action	66 area	29 bird	47 carried
60 actual	22 aren't	8 black	45 carry
60 actually	55 argue	33 blew	46 carrying
58 addition	57 argument	53 blood	28 case
46 address	16 arm	31 blow	37 catch
64 affect	17 around	18 blue	42 caught
32 afraid	16 art	38 board	38 center
54 after	54 article	30 body	53 central
30 afternoon	4 as	18 both	49 certain
32 again	4 ask	34 bottom	49 certainly
32 against	19 asked	41 bought	54 character
11 age	1 at	18 boy	27 cheat
32 air	11 ate	39 bread	8 check
9 all	58 attention	34 break	33 chief
52 all right	52 August	34 breakfast	20 child
29 allow	50 aunt	54 bridge	55 children
46 almost	57 author	67 brilliant	44 chocolate
46 alone	13 away	26 bring	30 choose
26 along	38 awful	14 broke	14 chose
46 already	23 awhile	50 brother	44 circle
46 although	8 back	41 brought	45 city
46 always	55 barely	29 brown	8 class
1 am	10 be	56 build	28 clean
40 America	30 bear	56 building	26 clear
40 American	47 beautiful	56 built	53 climb
20 among	45 beauty	47 business	53 climbed
1 an	24 became		53 climbing

8 clock	60 definitely	47 easiest	32 fair
14 close	69 delicious	27 east	67 familiar
49 clothes	64 describe	27 easy	47 families
20 cold	64 description	27 eat	45 family
66 college	51 destroy	54 edge	16 far
14 come	64 develop	64 education	69 fascinate
36 coming	59 development	64 effect	53 fasten
66 commit	6 did	62 eight	50 father
65 committee	22 didn't	62 either	44 favorite
60 complete	33 die	49 eleven	52 February
60 completely	33 died	48 else	15 feel
64 concentrate	61 difference	65 embarrass	19 feeling
69 conscience	61 different	5 end	5 felt
69 conscious	63 difficult	45 enemy	33 few
64 continue	36 dining	51 enjoy	33 field
69 continuous	34 dinner	41 enough	40 fight
66 control	58 direction	49 entertain	58 figure
61 convenient	29 dirty	66 equipped	9 fill
30 copy	65 disappear	63 escape	19 filled
38 corner	65 disappoint	55 especially	55 final
7 cost	69 discipline	56 etc.	55 finally
21 could	68 discuss	18 even	20 find
47 countries	68 discussion	18 evening	12 fire
45 country	63 disease	21 ever	29 first
42 course	67 distance	21 every	9 five
50 cousin	10 do	37 everyone	10 fly
38 cover	57 doctor	37 everything	31 follow
47 cries	19 does	37 everywhere	30 food
67 criticism	22 doesn't	65 exaggerate	18 foot
67 criticize	7 dog	59 example	17 for
10 cry	19 doing	59 excellent	54 force
19 crying	58 dollar	59 except	62 foreign
7 cut	22 don't	59 excite	51 forest
16 dark	14 done	59 excitement	25 forget
50 daughter	53 doubt	59 exciting	49 forty
13 day	29 down	59 excuse	17 found
39 dead	24 draw	59 exercise	21 four
26 dear	7 drop	61 existence	42 fourth
39 death	35 dropped	59 expect	15 free
62 deceive	35 dropping	59 experience	43 Friday
52 December	43 during	59 explain	41 friend
68 decide	51 duty	60 extremely	20 from
68 decided	27 each	30 eye	20 front
68 decision	47 earlier	11 face	9 full
15 deep	39 early	24 fact	43 further
60 definite	39 earth	32 fail	11 game

9 gave	39 head	61 independent
60 generally	26 hear	63 innocent
5 get	39 heard	25 inside
35 getting	33 heart	39 instead
29 girl	39 heavy	61 intelligent
9 give	62 height	57 interest
36 giving	18 hello	57 interesting
10 go	5 help	25 into
19 goes	16 her	6 is
19 going	13 here	56 island
14 gone	40 high	2 it
18 good	6 him	22 it's
18 goodbye	25 himself	22 its
3 got	6 his	25 itself
34 gotten	14 home	52 January
59 government	14 hope	69 jealous
35 grabbed	36 hoping	66 journal
11 grade	35 hopping	52 July
62 grammar	17 horse	52 June
50 grandfather	51 hospital	7 just
50 grandma	7 hot	15 keep
13 gray	17 hour	5 kept
34 great	17 house	56 key
15 green	29 how	20 kind
17 ground	29 however	33 knew
41 group	69 humorous	31 know
31 grow	49 hundred	54 knowledge
63 guarantee	45 hungry	31 known
56 guard	47 hurried	32 laid
56 guess	45 hurry	56 language
56 guilty	46 hurrying	16 large
57 gym	43 hurt	4 last
4 had	2 I	38 later
32 hair	22 I'll	42 laugh
53 half	22 I'm	42 laughed
4 hand	48 idea	42 laughter
42 handwriting	64 identify	13 lay
34 happen	2 if	28 lead
34 happened	64 imagine	28 leader
47 happiness	60 immediate	39 learn
45 happy	60 immediately	39 learned
16 hard	44 important	27 least
4 has	54 impossible	27 leave
9 have	2 in	5 led
22 haven't	63 incident	62 leisure
10 he	61 independence	26 length

8 less
46 lesson
5 let
53 let's
22 library
52 library
33 lie
5 life
44 lie
40 light
61 lightning
12 like
36 liked
20 line
6 list
53 listen
53 listened
37 little
9 live
36 lived
36 living
46 lonely
18 long
20 look
19 looked
30 loose
23 lose
7 lot
14 love
31 low
8 luck
47 luckily
45 lucky
66 machine
11 made
61 magazine
32 main
11 make
36 making
4 man
21 many
34 March
52 matter
13 may
52 May
25 maybe
10 me
28 mean

58 meant
50 measure
39 medicine
40 meet
15 men
12 middle
49 might
10 mile
49 million
48 mind
37 mine
51 minute
3 mischievous
67 miss
14 misspell
3 modern
51 Monday
48 money
48 month
37 moon
49 more
10 morning
57 most
20 mother
18 motor
26 mountain
19 move
30 moving
23 Mr.
7 Ms.
14 much
31 music
8 must
47 my
45 name
66 national
11 near
10 necessary
7 need
61 neighbor
32 neither
11 nephew
36 nervous
62 never
21 new
24 next
5 nice

32 nickel
65 niece
50 night
16 nine
49 nineteen
8 ninety
37 no
61 nobody
57 noise
48 noisy
48 north
51 northern
3 not
67 note
14 nothing
9 notice
52 November
29 now
68 occasion
66 occur
33 occurred
66 occurrence
32 occurring
4 October
17 of
8 off
48 office
13 often
17 oh
39 old
27 on
58 once
63 one
48 only
48 open
53 opinion
65 opportunity
65 opposite
17 or
20 other
8 our
17 out
25 outside
24 over
31 own
11 page

63 paid
68 parallel
68 parents
48 part
41 particular
8 pass
56 passed
44 patient
63 pattern
67 pay
68 peculiar
44 people
68 perfect
67 perform
64 perhaps
48 period
25 person
58 physical
58 picture
34 pie
6 piece
12 place
32 plain
32 plan
27 planned
28 planning
13 play
19 played
67 playing
27 pleasant
28 please
62 pocket
62 poem
48 point
46 poison
48 poor
5 possess
54 possible
29 power
60 practical
60 practically
48 practice
51 prairie
64 prepare
64 repetition
45 pretty

12 price
43 principal
62 principle
31 rhythm
8 ridge
40 right
54 ring
38 road
56 room
54 rules
7 run
35 running
26 safety
37 said
44 sale
11 same
65 sandwich
43 pronunciation
64 perhaps
44 promise
68 progress
13 program
55 professor
35 profession
7 procedure
44 problem
56 probably
38 privilege
40 private
48 prison
47 prettier
64 repeat
44 remember
51 relief
50 relative
56 several

63 restaurant
31 return
21 show
18 shown
7 stop
5 stopped
25 stopping
21 two
57 tying
38 type
24 uncle
50 understand
23 under
23 until
23 unless
23 whole
23 upon
12 us
9 will
6 win
38 window
36 winter
6 wish
60 usually
60 usual
16 war
21 wreck
42 write
55 writer
55 writing
42 written
24 word
24 work
16 world
42 wrong
42 wrote
31 year
26 yellow
5 yes
38 yesterday
8 you
22 you're
41 young
40 your
8 (your state)

9 should
54 stomach
6 the
23 their
23 them
23 themselves
58 see
37 somewhere
44 surprised
43 sure
10 to
36 today
36 this
7 up
25 very
60 view
21 voice
38 wait
38 voice
55 women
55 woman
25 wonder
23 wonderful
6 use
38 used to
31 using
40 Tuesday
43 turn
49 twelve
23 when
23 where
23 whether
23 which
23 white
23 while
22 weren't
23 what
13 we
10 week
15 weather
39 Wednesday
30 wear
27 weak
42 water
42 watch
42 was
42 warm

First   Second   Third

List 14
1. home
2. hope
3. note
4. chose
5. close
6. those
7. broke
8. love
9. above
10. some
11. come
12. one
13. done
14. gone
15. use

List 13
1. day
2. may
3. pay
4. lay
5. way
6. away
7. gray
8. play
9. stay
10. say
11. said
12. were
13. here
14. there
15. these

List 12
1. time
2. nine
3. line
4. shine
5. nice
6. price
7. life
8. quite
9. like
10. mile
11. smile
12. fire
13. wide
14. side
15. size

List 11
1. came
2. same
3. name
4. game
5. ate
6. state
7. age
8. page
9. take
10. make
11. made
12. grade
13. sale
14. face
15. place

List 10
1. go
2. no
3. so
4. do
5. to
6. be
7. he
8. me
9. we
10. she
11. by
12. my
13. try
14. cry
15. fly

List 9
1. all
2. call
3. small
4. well
5. tell
6. fill
7. will
8. still
9. full
10. have
11. gave
12. give
13. live
14. five
15. move

List 8
1. back
2. black
3. check
4. sick
5. clock
6. luck
7. quick
8. off
9. class
10. pass
11. less
12. miss
13. you
14. your
15. our

List 7
1. hot
2. lot
3. dog
4. cost
5. stop
6. drop
7. us
8. up
9. but
10. cut
11. run
12. just
13. must
14. much
15. such

List 6
1. is
2. his
3. him
4. big
5. did
6. win
7. sit
8. quit
9. wish
10. with
11. list
12. this
13. the
14. they
15. are

List 5
1. let
2. get
3. yes
4. red
5. led
6. men
7. end
8. went
9. then
10. them
11. best
12. felt
13. help
14. next
15. kept

List 4
1. and
2. can
3. plan
4. hand
5. stand
6. man
7. than
8. that
9. last
10. as
11. ask
12. had
13. has
14. was
15. a

List 1
1. am
2. an
3. at

List 25
1. itself
2. himself
3. themselves
4. into
5. upon
6. forget
7. maybe
8. cannot
9. today
10. inside
11. outside
12. without
13. understand
14. another
15. put

List 24
1. act
2. fact
3. saw
4. draw
5. work
6. word
7. world
8. only
9. open
10. over
11. under
12. after
13. become
14. became
15. welcome

List 23
1. who
2. who's
3. whose
4. lose
5. why
6. what
7. when
8. where
9. which
10. whether
11. white
12. while
13. awhile
14. whole
15. more

List 22
1. its
2. it's
3. that's
4. let's
5. I'll
6. I'm
7. they're
8. you're
9. can't
10. don't
11. didn't
12. doesn't
13. aren't
14. weren't
15. haven't

List 21
1. once
2. four
3. two
4. six
5. seven
6. any
7. many
8. never
9. ever
10. every
11. very
12. would
13. could
14. should
15. shall

List 20
1. old
2. cold
3. told
4. both
5. most
6. find
7. mind
8. kind
9. child
10. second
11. month
12. among
13. front
14. from
15. other

List 19
1. asked
2. called
3. looked
4. played
5. stayed
6. filled
7. doing
8. going
9. playing
10. trying
11. crying
12. being
13. feeling
14. goes
15. does

List 18
1. took
2. look
3. book
4. stood
5. foot
6. good
7. goodbye
8. hello
9. even
10. evening
11. morning
12. blue
13. true
14. boy
15. their

List 17
1. or
2. for
3. north
4. short
5. horse
6. house
7. out
8. about
9. around
10. found
11. ground
12. south
13. hour
14. oh
15. of

List 16
1. car
2. far
3. dark
4. hard
5. arm
6. warm
7. war
8. art
9. part
10. start
11. large
12. talk
13. walk
14. want
15. her

List 15
1. free
2. three
3. see
4. seem
5. seen
6. green
7. deep
8. sleep
9. keep
10. street
11. meet
12. week
13. feel
14. need
15. been

List 2
1. I
2. if
3. in
4. it

List 36
1. tired
2. scared
3. liked
4. lived
5. used to
6. using
7. shining
8. dining
9. taking
10. making
11. moving
12. giving
13. living
14. hoping
15. coming

List 35
1. stepped
2. slipped
3. grabbed
4. planned
5. planning
6. dropped
7. dropping
8. stopped
9. stopping
10. hopping
11. getting
12. running
13. sledding
14. swimming
15. beginning

List 34
1. better
2. matter
3. gotten
4. dinner
5. summer
6. sudden
7. happen
8. happened
9. suppose
10. supposed to
11. bottom
12. great
13. break
14. breakfast
15. quiet

List 33
1. new
2. knew
3. few
4. blew
5. threw
6. view
7. die
8. died
9. lie
10. believe
11. pie
12. piece
13. field
14. chief
15. heart

List 32
1. wait
2. waiting
3. rain
4. plain
5. main
6. paid
7. laid
8. fail
9. again
10. against
11. air
12. fair
13. hair
14. afraid
15. raise

List 31
1. own
2. know
3. known
4. show
5. shown
6. blow
7. slow
8. grow
9. throw
10. low
11. below
12. follow
13. yellow
14. window
15. tomorrow

List 30
1. too
2. loose
3. food
4. moon
5. soon
6. room
7. smooth
8. school
9. afternoon
10. choose
11. eye
12. body
13. copy
14. wear
15. bear

List 29
1. now
2. how
3. however
4. down
5. brown
6. town
7. allow
8. power
9. dirty
10. bird
11. girl
12. third
13. first
14. begin
15. began

List 28
1. sea
2. season
3. reason
4. lead
5. leader
6. clean
7. team
8. mean
9. meant
10. read
11. ready
12. case
13. care
14. scare
15. animal

List 27
1. weak
2. speak
3. each
4. reach
5. teach
6. teacher
7. eat
8. cheat
9. easy
10. east
11. least
12. please
13. leave
14. real
15. really

List 26
1. along
2. long
3. length
4. strong
5. strength
6. spring
7. bring
8. thing
9. think
10. thank you
11. year
12. near
13. hear
14. dear
15. clear

List 3
1. on
2. not
3. got

Fourth

List 37
1. nobody
2. nothing
3. anyway
4. anybody
5. everyone
6. everything
7. everywhere
8. somebody
9. something
10. somewhere
11. sometimes
12. catch
13. watch
14. stretch
15. little

List 38
1. cover
2. later
3. center
4. corner
5. water
6. winter
7. wonder
8. wonderful
9. careful
10. awful
11. until
12. yesterday
13. type
14. road
15. board

List 39
1. weather
2. measure
3. heavy
4. head
5. bread
6. dead
7. death
8. instead
9. pleasant
10. search
11. heard
12. early
13. earth
14. learn
15. learned

List 40
1. fight
2. light
3. might
4. night
5. right
6. tight
7. high
8. touch
9. young
10. group
11. before
12. because
13. between
14. private
15. friend

List 41
1. bought
2. brought
3. thought
4. though
5. through
6. enough
7. tough
8. rough
9. laugh
10. laughed
11. laughter
12. caught
13. taught
14. course
15. fourth

List 42
1. write
2. writer
3. writing
4. handwriting
5. wrote
6. wrong
7. wreck
8. terrible
9. turn
10. return
11. important
12. during
13. further
14. problem
15. sugar

List 43
1. Sunday
2. Monday
3. Tuesday
4. Wednesday
5. Thursday
6. Friday
7. Saturday
8. study
9. sorry
10. carry
11. hurry
12. surprise
13. program
14. family
15. promise

List 44
1. circle
2. city
3. story
4. people
5. enemy
6. hungry
7. country
8. lucky
9. address
10. happy
11. pretty
12. happiness
13. business
14. beauty
15. beautiful

List 45
1. busy
2. almost
3. already
4. although
5. across
6. alone
7. lonely
8. lesson
9. recess
10. unless
11. earlier
12. easiest
13. prettier
14. luckily
15. studying

List 46
1. always
2. almost
3. already
4. stories
5. families
6. tried
7. hurried
8. carried
9. studied
10. hurrying
11. carrying
12. happiness
13. business
14. addition
15. attention

List 47
1. cries
2. countries
3. families
4. stories
5. tried
6. hurried
7. carried
8. studied
9. nervous
10. serious
11. continuous
12. action
13. direction
14. delicious
15. appreciate

Fifth

List 48
1. noise
2. noisy
3. point
4. voice
5. poison
6. prison
7. person
8. period
9. perhaps
10. perfect
11. else
12. idea
13. office
14. notice
15. practice

List 49
1. mountain
2. captain
3. certain
4. entertain
5. eleven
6. twelve
7. twenty-one
8. forty
9. nineteen
10. ninety
11. hundred
12. thousand
13. million
14. nephew
15. relative

List 50
1. sister
2. mother
3. brother
4. father
5. grandfather
6. grandma
7. daughter
8. son
9. parents
10. uncle
11. aunt
12. cousin
13. niece
14. nephew
15. relative

List 51
1. stairs
2. prairie
3. duty
4. rules
5. minute
6. secret
7. secretary
8. destroy
9. enjoy
10. hospital
11. forest
12. together
13. northern
14. modern
15. pattern

List 52
1. January
2. February
3. March
4. April
5. May
6. June
7. July
8. August
9. September
10. October
11. November
12. December
13. library
14. a lot
15. all right

List 53
1. sentence
2. often
3. fasten
4. listen
5. listened
6. final
7. finally
8. answer
9. half
10. doubt
11. climb
12. impossible
13. possible
14. since
15. medicine

List 54
1. ridge
2. bridge
3. edge
4. knowledge
5. ache
6. stomach
7. character
8. statement
9. tragedy
10. argue
11. central
12. poor
13. blood
14. safety
15. force

List 55
1. woman
2. women
3. children
4. language
5. probably
6. doctor
7. guess
8. guard
9. guilty
10. argument
11. truly
12. built
13. building
14. island
15. etc.

List 56
1. several
2. toward
3. author
4. motor
5. picture
6. figure
7. nickel
8. sign
9. key
10. money
11. gym
12. passed
13. straight
14. absent
15. bicycle

List 57
1. tie
2. tying
3. skiing
4. interest
5. interesting
6. regular
7. dollar
8. calendar
9. speech
10. question
11. direction
12. action
13. addition
14. attention
15. statement

List 58
1. sense
2. pocket
3. ticket
4. scene
5. principal
6. lesson
7. easiest
8. earlier
9. prettier
10. luckily
11. hurrying
12. carrying
13. studying
14. business
15. beautiful

Sixth

List 59
1. accept
2. except
3. excellent
4. excuse
5. excite
6. exciting
7. excitement
8. example
9. exercise
10. experience
11. explain
12. expect
13. develop
14. development
15. government

List 60
1. carefully
2. complete
3. completely
4. extremely
5. definite
6. definitely
7. benefit
8. actual
9. actually
10. usual
11. usually
12. practical
13. generally
14. immediate
15. immediately

List 61
1. music
2. misspell
3. magazine
4. lightning
5. opinion
6. either
7. neither
8. benefit
9. different
10. difference
11. independent
12. intelligent
13. patient
14. reference
15. convenient

List 62
1. eight
2. weight
3. height
4. neighbor
5. leisure
6. difficult
7. either
8. neither
9. guarantee
10. receive
11. receipt
12. seize
13. weird
14. foreign
15. rhythm

List 63
1. affect
2. effect
3. suggest
4. accidentally
5. prepare
6. continue
7. appear
8. recommend
9. control
10. realize
11. recognize
12. criticize
13. occasion
14. criticism
15. perform

List 64
1. incident
2. accident
3. necessary
4. escape
5. innocent
6. difficult
7. concentrate
8. guarantee
9. deceive
10. procedure
11. exaggerate
12. education
13. disappear
14. disappoint
15. occur

List 65
1. approach
2. opportunity
3. achieve
4. relief
5. appear
6. imagine
7. disappoint
8. occur
9. occurred
10. occurring
11. occurrence
12. describe
13. description
14. national
15. distance

List 66
1. college
2. privilege
3. necessary
4. achieve
5. recommend
6. commit
7. guarantee
8. exaggerate
9. accommodate
10. committee
11. embarrass
12. referred
13. equipped
14. journal
15. arctic

List 67
1. summary
2. apology
3. apologize
4. realize
5. recognize
6. criticize
7. criticism
8. acquaint
9. distance
10. acquaintance
11. professor
12. appearance
13. brilliant
14. peculiar
15. familiar

List 68
1. principle
2. principal
3. physical
4. decide
5. decided
6. decision
7. occasion
8. success
9. succeed
10. professor
11. possess
12. progress
13. discuss
14. sandwich
15. discussion

List 69
1. scene
2. fascinate
3. discipline
4. scissors
5. science
6. conscience
7. conscious
8. nervous
9. jealous
10. serious
11. humorous
12. continuous
13. delicious
14. mischievous
15. appreciate

Homophones*

- accept – except
- access – excess
- ad – add
- addition – edition
- affect – effect
- allowed – aloud
- ant – aunt
- are – our
- ate – eight
- be – bee
- bear – bare
- beat – beet
- berry – bury
- blew – blue
- board – bored
- break – brake
- buy – by
- buy – by – bye
- capital – capitol
- ceiling – sealing
- celery – salary
- cell – sell
- cent – sent
- cent – sent – scent
- cereal – serial
- chews – choose
- clothes – close
- conscience – conscious
- council – counsel
- course – coarse
- creak – creek
- dear – deer

- desert – dessert
- dew – do – due
- die – dye
- fair – fare
- fir – fur
- flew – flu
- flour – flower
- for – four
- form – from
- forth – fourth
- great – grate
- groan – grown
- guessed – guest
- hair – hare
- hall – haul
- hay – hey
- heal – heel
- hear – here
- heard – herd
- higher – hire
- hole – whole
- horse – hoarse
- hour – our
- I – eye
- its – it's
- lead – led
- loose – lose
- maid – made
- mail – male
- main – mane
- meat – meet
- missed – mist

- new – knew
- night – knight
- no – know
- none – nun
- nose – knows
- not – knot
- off – of
- oh – owe
- one – won
- pail – pale
- pain – pane
- pair – pare – pear
- passed – past
- patience – patients
- pause – paws
- peace – piece
- peak – peek
- peal – peel
- plain – plane
- principal – principle
- profit – prophet
- quite – quiet
- rain – rein – reign
- raise – rays
- rap – wrap
- read – red
- reads – reeds
- real – reel
- right – write
- ring – wring
- road – rode
- sail – sale
- scene – seen

- sea – see
- seam – seem
- sense – since
- sew – so – sow
- soar – sore
- some – sum
- son – sun
- stairs – stares
- stationary – stationery
- steak – stake
- steal – steel
- tacks – tax
- tail – tale
- then – than
- there – their
- there – they're – their
- threw – through
- to – two
- to – too – two
- toad – towed
- toes – tows
- wade – weighed
- waist – waste
- wait – weight
- way – weigh
- weak – week
- weather – whether
- were – we're
- where – were
- which – witch
- whose – who's
- would – wood
- your – you're

*Worksheets and lessons for teaching each of these sets of
homophones are in the *Homophones Resource Book*.

Capitalization (see pp. 39–52)

- first word of sentence
- titles of books
- names of magazines
- names of newspapers
- titles of stories
- titles of chapters
- titles of poems
- titles of plays
- titles of TV shows
- titles of movies
- titles of songs
- titles of paintings
- first names of people
- initials
- surnames of people

- pet names
- nationalities and
  languages
- names of religions
- names of political
  groups
- groups, organizations,
  clubs, businesses
- continents
- countries
- geographical regions
  (not directions)
- states and provinces
- postal abbreviations
- cities and towns

- streets, highways,
  roads, avenues, etc.
- parks
- oceans and seas
- bays and other bodies
  of water
- rivers
- creeks, brooks, etc.
- waterfalls
- lakes
- mountains and
  mountain ranges
- valleys, canyons
- caves, caverns
- forests

- islands
- deserts and other
  geographical features
- heavenly bodies
- bridges
- schools, colleges
- stores
- museums
- hospitals, churches,
  hotels, motels
- libraries
- restaurants
- other man-made
  structures
- holidays

Punctuation (see pp. 53–54)

Period
- ❏ to end statements
- ❏ to end commands
- ❏ after initials
- ❏ after abbreviations

Question Mark
- ❏ to end questions

Exclamation Mark
- ❏ to end exclamations

Apostrophe
- ❏ in contractions
- ❏ to show possession
- ❏ to show plural possession
  (boys' hats)

Hyphen
- ❏ in writing numbers from
  twenty-one to *ninety-nine*

Comma
- ❏ between day and date
- ❏ between date and year
- ❏ between city and state
- ❏ between city and country
- ❏ between items in a series
- ❏ after words which introduce a sentence
  - ❏ yes
  - ❏ oh
  - ❏ no
  - ❏ well
  - ❏ first
- ❏ before certain words which end a sentence
  - ❏ too
  - ❏ also
  - ❏ etc.
- ❏ in direct address
  - ❏ *Mom, are you ready?*
  - ❏ *I understand, Mr. Jones.*
  - ❏ *This, Mike, is for you.*
- ❏ in a compound sentence
  - ❏ before *and*
  - ❏ before *but*
  - ❏ before *or*
- ❏ in tag questions: *He's here, isn't he?*
- ❏ to separate parenthetical phrases
  - ❏ for example
  - ❏ for instance
  - ❏ in fact
  - ❏ in one case
  - ❏ furthermore
  - ❏ in addition
  - ❏ also
  - ❏ meanwhile
  - ❏ at last
  - ❏ in the meantime
  - ❏ to begin with
  - ❏ at this point
  - ❏ at the same time
  - ❏ in conclusion
  - ❏ as a result
  - ❏ therefore
  - ❏ for this reason
  - ❏ on the other hand
  - ❏ however
  - ❏ nevertheless

Word Building (see pp. 55–62)

Suffixes
- ❏ *-able, -ible*
- ❏ *-al*
- ❏ *-en*
- ❏ *-er (worker)*
- ❏ *-er, -est*
- ❏ *-ful*
- ❏ *-hood*
- ❏ *-ish*
- ❏ *-ity, -ty*
- ❏ *-ty (sixty)*
- ❏ *-ize*
- ❏ *-less*
- ❏ *-ly*
- ❏ *-ment*
- ❏ *-ness*
- ❏ *-ion, -tion, -ation*
- ❏ *-y*

Prefixes
- ❏ *de-*
- ❏ *dis-*
- ❏ *en-, em-*
- ❏ *in-, im-, ir-, il-*
- ❏ *inter-*
- ❏ *mis-*
- ❏ *out-*
- ❏ *over-*
- ❏ *pre-*
- ❏ *re-*
- ❏ *un-*
- ❏ *under-*

Grammar (see pp. 63–76)

Nouns
- ❏ definition of noun
- ❏ common & proper nouns
- ❏ singular & plural nouns
- ❏ mass & count nouns
- ❏ possessive nouns

Pronouns
- ❏ definition of pronoun
- ❏ personal pronouns
- ❏ first, second, third person
- ❏ subject pronouns
- ❏ object pronouns
- ❏ possessive pronouns
- ❏ indefinite pronouns
- ❏ reflexive pronouns

Adjectives
- ❏ definition of adjective
- ❏ articles *(a, an, the)*
- ❏ comparative adjectives
- ❏ superlative adjectives

Verbs
- ❏ definition of verb
- ❏ action verbs
- ❏ verbs expressing state of being
- ❏ auxiliary verbs
- ❏ infinitives and use of *to*
- ❏ present tense
- ❏ past tense
- ❏ future tense
- ❏ irregular verb formations

Adverbs
- ❏ definition of adverb
- ❏ adverbs telling where
- ❏ adverbs telling when
- ❏ adverbs telling how
- ❏ adverbs telling to what extent (intensifiers)

Prepositions
- ❏ definition of preposition

Conjunctions
- ❏ definition of conjunction
- ❏ coordinating conjunctions
- ❏ subordinating conjunctions

Interjections
- ❏ definition of interjection

Letter Form (see pp. 36–37)

- ❏ Correct placement of parts of letter.
- ❏ Return address.
  - ❏ Street address — common abbreviations with periods.
  - ❏ City, comma, state.
  - ❏ Zip code.
- ❏ Date, comma, year.
- ❏ Greeting, comma.
- ❏ Body. Indent paragraphs.
- ❏ Closing, comma.
  - ❏ Spelling of *truly.*
  - ❏ Spelling of *sincerely.*
- ❏ Signature
- ❏ Proper use of P.S. (post script)

- ❏ How to fold a letter correctly.
- ❏ Return address.
  - ❏ Name of sender.
  - ❏ Street address.
  - ❏ City, comma, state, zip.
  - ❏ *No date on the envelope.*
- ❏ Placement of address.
- ❏ Placement of stamp.

Outline Form (see p. 38)

- ❏ Roman numerals.
- ❏ Headings, subheadings, etc.
- ❏ Indenting properly.

Usage (see p. 67)

- ❏ bring – take
- ❏ can – may
- ❏ did – done
- ❏ doesn't – don't
- ❏ good – well
- ❏ in – into
- ❏ lay – lie
- ❏ learn – teach
- ❏ leave – let
- ❏ lend – borrow
- ❏ raise – rise
- ❏ set – sit

Quotations & Dialogue (see p. 54)

- ❏ Quotation marks to enclose exact words.
- ❏ Capitalize first word of speaker's sentence.
- ❏ Capitalize first word of writer's sentence.
- ❏ Comma to separate quote from "she said" and similar phrases.
  - ❏ *"You are my friend," she said.*
  - ❏ *She said, "You are my friend."*
  - ❏ *"You," she said, "are my friend."*
- ❏ Alternatives to the word *said,* from list to the right.
- ❏ Question marks in quotations.
  - ❏ *"Who are you?" she asked.*
- ❏ Exclamation point in quotations.
  - ❏ *"Look out!" he yelled.*
- ❏ Dialogue. Begin new paragraph for each speaker.

Bibliographic Form (see p. 38)

- ❏ Form: hanging indent.
- ❏ Leave out information not available.

Book
- ❏ Author's last name, comma, first name, period.
- ❏ Title of book, underlined, period.
- ❏ City of publication, colon, publisher, comma, year of publication, period.

Magazine
- ❏ Author's last name, comma, first name, period.
- ❏ Title of article in quotation marks, period.
- ❏ Name of magazine underlined, number of volume, month and date of issue in parentheses, colon, page numbers, period.

Encyclopedia
- ❏ Author's last name, comma, first name, period.
- ❏ Title of article in quotation marks, period.
- ❏ Name of encyclopedia underlined, period.
- ❏ Year of publication, period.

announced
answered
asked
commanded
demanded
drawled
echoed
exclaimed
giggled
growled
grumbled
hissed
howled
insisted
laughed
chuckled
moaned
mumbled
murmured
muttered
ordered
pleaded
protested
remarked
repeated
replied
roared
screamed
shouted
sighed
snapped
snarled
squeaked
squealed
stammered
stated
whimpered
whined
whispered
yelled

Dictation Sentences

Teacher _____   Week of _____

Teach or emphasize the following:

❒ Spelling words from list _____

Choose a specific objective to teach or emphasize in one or two of the following areas:

❒ Homophones _____   ❒ Usage _____

❒ Capitalization_____   ❒ Punctuation _____

❒ Prefix or suffix _____   ❒ Grammar _____

❒ Form _____   ❒ Other _____

Monday

1. _____
2. _____
3. _____
4. _____

Tuesday

1. _____
2. _____
3. _____
4. _____

Wednesday

1. _____
2. _____
3. _____
4. _____

Thursday

1. _____
2. _____
3. _____
4. _____

Friday

1. _____
2. _____
3. _____
4. _____

DICTATION SENTENCES

No one is more qualified than the teacher to analyze the current needs of a particular group of students, and to decide which language objective should be taught at any point in time and for how long it should be reviewed. Sound decisions concerning what to teach and when to teach it must be based primarily on needs that are apparent in student writing.

For these reasons, teachers are in the best position to write dictation sentences for their own students. Any set of sentences prepared by someone else will have limitations, primarily the restriction of flexibility, one of dictation's primary benefits. A complete set of prepared sentences could hurry teachers into introducing new objectives before they feel their students are ready, assume prerequisite knowledge that students don't have, or provide too much or too little review.

Nevertheless, *any* dictation is better than none, and I want to make it easy for you the teacher to begin using this powerful method so that you can see results for yourself. For these reasons, I've written a "starter set" of sentences, one to follow each *Spelling Plus* list except the kindergarten lists. These sentences include all spelling words from the previous spelling list, as well as some words in patterns students have studied. A very few words that have not specifically been taught, but which students should be able to spell, are italicized to alert you that some students may not know them. Twenty sentences have been prepared for each of lists 4–47, and ten sentences for each of lists 48–69. Any of the sentences can be dictated at any time after the spelling list has been taught, but it's best to dictate them the week following spelling instruction. Upper-grade teachers can use sentences from lower-grade lists for review.

Once you are accustomed to the daily routine of dictation and begin to see improvement in student writing, you will likely be very motivated to invest the planning time necessary to write your own, tailor-made sentences. Although it's ideal to have excellent, sensible, realistic sentences and paragraphs, it is more important to include many elements students need to practice. The emphasis in dictation is on *form,* not content.

Read exclamations with *lots* of expression, so there is no doubt that you're dictating an exclamation!!!

To teach paragraph form, introduced after list 17 on the following pages, have students:

1. Place two fingers to the right of the red margin line. Begin the first sentence at that point. This is called "indenting" the paragraph.
2. Do not start a new line for a new sentence within a paragraph. Leave about the width of one finger between sentences and continue writing on the same line.
3. When you come to the red margin line that shows through from the other side of the paper, finish the word you're writing and write the next word on the next line, starting at the red margin line. Do not squeeze words on the line. If a word is too long to fit on a line, put the entire word on the next line. You will eventually learn to judge whether you can fit another very short word on the line, but to be safe, it's best to just go to the next line.
4. Do not divide words. The rules for correct hyphenation are quite complex, and there is no real need for hyphenation in student writing.

After List 4

1. I can ask that man.
2. Dan was not in.
3. Jan has a hot hand.
4. I had a plan at last.

5. The rat was not as fat as the cat.
6. Ron and I can stand on it.
7. I am not a man.
8. Don and Dan can ask.

9. Sam has that last can.
10. It was not as hot.
11. A man got in at last.
12. That was a bad plan.

13. That man can not stand.
14. Ron and I got it.
15. A man was last.
16. Jan can plan that.

17. I can stand if Sam can not stand.
18. Jan had a bad hand.
19. Ask if Ron has a plan.
20. Don is a fast man.

Capitalize names.
Capitalize beginning of sentence.
Period at end of statement.

After List 5

1. Dan was best.
2. Sam was next.
3. Jan was last.
4. Ron kept a can.

5. I can let it stand.
6. Jan led them.
7. That was best.
8. I can get help.

9. Then let it end.
10. I had a red can.
11. It is best to plan.
12. I went next.

13. Ron felt hot.
14. A man led them on.
15. Red was best.
16. A man went to help them at last.

17. Yes, I can get them.
18. Yes, a man kept it.
19. Yes, I went next.
20. Yes, Don has a plan.

Comma after "yes."

After List 6

1. Yes, they are with him.
2. Yes, this list is big.
3. Yes, his wish is to win.
4. The men did not sit.

5. Dan can not quit.
6. Yes, his wish list is red.
7. Yes, that big man can get it.
8. Yes, Sam was with him.

9. Yes, this is the best.
10. The men went last.
11. Yes, they are next to him.
12. I did not quit.

13. The last plan is the best.
14. Yes, I can ask them to help.
15. They led him to the end.
16. Sam did not quit.

17. I can sit with them.
18. Yes, they are his men.
19. The last list was the best.
20. They did not win.

After List 7

1. That big dog is hot.
2. Yes, this cost us a lot.
3. I must stop to cut this.
4. Dan can run with us.

5. This was such a big help.
6. Yes, they did just as much.
7. I ran but I did not win.
8. Sam went up with the men.

9. They just had a drop.
10. It was such a big cut.
11. His dog cost him a lot.
12. They just can not quit.

13. Jan went with the next man.
14. I must stop that big dog.
15. Yes, they wish to win.
16. They can not win if they quit.

17. Drop this list with him.
18. Yes, I was led up to get it.
19. Dan felt the best.
20. Cut just as much as they did.

After List 8

1. They went back to check on the class.
2. Your luck was bad.
3. I miss our big clock.
4. Yes, you can sit with him.

5. Are you sick?
6. Did our class pass?
7. Was Ron quick?
8. Do you want less than that?

9. Can you cut this off?
10. Is your black dog sick?
11. Did you miss us?
12. Can they ask that man?

13. Was that man the best?
14. Can you run back with us?
15. Did you check it off your list?
16. Can I help them win?

17. Did they get sick then?
18. Was Don the last man to stand?
19. Is this your big list?
20. Can I sit with our class?

Question mark after a question.

After List 9

1. Did they all pass?
2. Did the plan help you?
3. Will you tell the class?
4. Can you fill this small can?

5. Can you give this check to Don?
6. Yes, I can give that check to Don.
7. Are they still with the men?
8. Yes, they are still with the men.

9. Will you call the class?
10. Yes, I will call the class.
11. Can Don move that clock?
12. Yes, Don can move that clock.

13. Did Bill still have a full can?
14. Yes, Bill still had a full can.
15. Did they run well?
16. Yes, they ran well.

17. Can all five of them pass?
18. Yes, all five of them can pass.
19. Did they give him a big check?
20. Yes, they gave him a big check.

Questions and answers.

After List 10

1. Will you try to help me?
2. Yes, I will try to help you.
3. Do you plan to ask him?
4. No, I do not plan to ask him.

5. Can he fly with our men?
6. Yes, he can fly with our men.
7. Will she be the best?
8. No, she will not be the best.

9. Can we help your sick dog?
10. No, you can not help my sick dog.
11. Did she go to check the clock?
12. Yes, she went to check the clock.

13. Did she cry a lot?
14. They kept a list by the bed.
15. Can you go with us?
16. They are all so sick.

17. We have a small class.
18. Can she stand up?
19. They gave me so much to do.
20. Do they have to fly?

Two types of sentences.
Comma after "no."

After List 11

1. Is this the place?
2. Can you name this game?
3. It will cost less at the sale.
4. She got a bad grade.

5. They ate so much!
6. A man came to take our dog!
7. You made a bad face!
8. They are all the same age!

9. You must be quick!
10. I can make it with you!
11. This is such a small page!
12. They like this state a lot!

13. This is my best grade!
14. We quit!
15. I felt so sick!
16. I can do just as much as you!

17. This is the best sale!
18. Is your face hot?
19. Yes, my face is hot.
20. Sam will stop at our place.

Exclamations and exclamation mark.

After List 12

1. You are so nice!
2. I like your smile!
3. This line is quite wide!
4. Is this my size?

5. We went nine miles.
6. Can you tell me the time?
7. The fire makes your face shine.
8. Our side is the best!

9. This price is not bad!
10. He had a lot of luck in his life.
11. Are they all on my side?
12. Yes, they are all on your side.

13. You will pass if you try.
14. That fire is hot!
15. Do you plan to fly?
16. Can you check back with me?

17. We had quite a nice time!
18. Do you have size nine?
19. They will miss the game.
20. I still have your black hat.

Three types of sentences.

After List 13

1. This may not be the best way.
2. Can you stay here with me?
3. These are nice!
4. She said we have to pay the price.

5. It was a gray day.
6. We must run a mile to get there!
7. The man went away with a smile.
8. Will you play a game with me?

9. Do not be quick to quit.
10. Stand tall and you will win.
11. Say your name and age.
12. Lay that by the fire.

13. Tell me if they were here.
14. Do not cry if you can help it.
15. Go to the end of the line.
16. Go away and play with Jan.

17. Ask him if he can stay.
18. Pay the man so we can go.
19. Give them as much as they like.
20. Call them to ask if they can drop by.

Commands end with a period.

After List 14

1. Stand still and do not move.
2. Ask if they were gray or black.
3. Try to pass him and then stop.
4. Do not give your list away.

5. I hope some of them are home.
6. Can you use one of these?
7. Come with us to the back.
8. I love you a lot!

9. Those dogs have gone away.
10. It broke above the line.
11. Are they all done with the note?
12. But I chose that size!

13. Close it if you wish.
14. Jan said you were here to stay.
15. No, we will move away one of these days.
16. I wish you a lot of luck!

17. Did you like my note?
18. Yes, it was quite nice.
19. They kept it at home by the fire.
20. I like life a lot!

Four types of sentences.

After List 15

1. Three of them are green and one is gray.
2. They seem to need more sleep this week.
3. We feel quite free here.
4. That man has not seen this place yet.

5. This is a nice street.
6. I will meet you at your place.
7. He said we can keep our dog here.
8. I can see that it is deep.

9. We have come to stay with you.
10. Some of them said to stop.
11. You can keep nine or ten.
12. She may try to run away.

13. He said the sale will be this week.
14. There were three men in the street.
15. The black dog came close to the fire.
16. Your smile is the best one.

17. I hope our class will line up fast.
18. Some of them went to call home.
19. She said to take the note with us.
20. I hope you can use some of these.

After List 16

1. It may be hard to find your car in the dark.
2. We want to start here.
3. Art is a nice part of life.
4. The next line is large.

5. Can you talk to her?
6. Do you want to walk with us?
7. Is your arm warm yet?
8. I hope the war will end.

9. Do you like to fly?
10. He said to close it!
11. We went on a walk with our class.
12. Can we start to play the game?

13. Do we have far to walk?
14. They have been here for some time!
15. Have you felt sick?
16. Mom said to come home by three.

17. Can you use some help this week?
18. Were they still here when you came?
19. Have you been with your class all day?
20. You will have to try to see her!

After List 17

My horse got out in the last hour. She ran around the house and off to the south. I had to call her and walk for about a mile! I found her at last on the next street.

Can you come to my house to play in about an hour? I have a game you will like. We can meet next to the large tree on your street so I can walk with you. Check with your mom and call me back.

Oh, no! I hope we chose a short way to get there. Do we need to go north or south? Can you find our map and check to see if we are lost?

It was the end of the day. The *sky* was not yet dark. It was warm and still. I sat on the ground and felt the nice green *grass*.

I need to talk with you about that big clock. The hour hand quit and no one can tell the time. Dan said you want to *fix* it and I can help. It will not cost much.

Paragraph form.
Comma after "oh."
See p. 17 for more on paragraph form.

Words in italics are not on the 1000 word core list.

After List 18

The men took a good look at our car. It did not start well at all. They had to check to see if they had the parts. They said to come back the next morning.

Oh, no! It is evening and we must start for home. Say goodbye to the boy you met. We will sleep and then come back about nine in the morning.

Did you see that boy who stood on one foot for an hour? Is it true that he is still here or has he gone away? My dad said he can even stand on his hands! Say hello for me if you see him.

Their big blue house is for sale. They want to move south to a warm place. I hope they will sell their old books. There is one book I just love and I can even pay for it.

I went home one morning last week. I did not feel well at all. It was such a nice day but I felt so sick! I had to get warm and try to sleep.

After List 19

My mom and I had a good talk last evening. I am doing my best but my grades are still not good. She said I need to stop playing around so much in class. She asked me if I wanted help and I said yes!

I called your house this morning but no one was home. I have been trying to find time to go for a walk with you. Does this evening sound good? I am going for a walk at about five and we can meet then if you want.

The boy was feeling bad. He was even crying! He had played well but he still lost. It is true that no one can win all the time!

We looked around for their small dog for days. We filled his dish and called him a lot. He has stayed away for a week. My mom said he must be gone for good.

Does your dad like being away so much? It seems like he goes on a lot of trips! We miss him quite a bit here. I hope he can stay home next week and see our big game!

After List 20

The child told both of us that he was in second grade. We helped him find his class. He looked like he felt like crying. But the other boys were kind and wanted him to play with them.

This has been a cold month! Most of us did not mind. We stayed in the house most of the time. It was nice and warm by the fire.

Have you found an old toy this morning? I have looked all around the house for it. It is green and blue. It may be out among those trees.

That old man does not have a job but he wants to help those in need. He is trying to find their lost dog. He goes from one place to the other calling for her. He walks from here to there and back.

1. Their books are among the best.
2. The second boy came to the front and started to talk.
3. Does your child mind playing out in the cold?
4. The man said to wish you a good morning!

After List 21

1. Their four boys run home every day.
2. Your horse is very large!
3. Does the bus stop here at seven?
4. Many of us would like to stay around all evening.
5. Could their two boys have the same name?
6. I called once at about six.
7. Should any of us go with their class?
8. There will never be a good war.
9. Shall we see if they are nice?
10. Every street there looks about the same.
11. Do not ever stop trying if you want to win.
12. Is that their dog out front?
13. They are walking here from their house.
14. I never want to say goodbye.
15. There were never any nice mornings there.
16. Their child could be six or seven.

There are two gray houses on their street. Their house is the second one. They would like to move up north at the end of the month. Their child wants to stay here for life!

After List 22

1. It's going to start above that hill.
2. That's the second time you have called in less than an hour!
3. They're quite glad that you chose that book.
4. Doesn't that boy have a nice smile?
5. Haven't you filled your glass?
6. We weren't feeling very well back then.
7. You didn't meet most of the boys in front.
8. We didn't even try to stop their horse.
9. You're doing very well.
10. Let's go see if they're home!
11. I'm going to have to say goodbye.
12. Don't you wish they could stay?
13. Its name is Sam.
14. It's the second pet he's ever had.
15. It's small but its feet are large.
16. He said its price was not bad.

I'll tell you about these cars. The green one in front broke last month. The second one doesn't run very well. They aren't good cars and I can't fix them.

Week 24 C-2   wk 2

After List 23

1. Why are you feeling so bad?
2. I can't see whether or not it's white.
3. Who went out with you last evening?
4. Which one of you wants to be in front?

5. When were you trying to call?
6. I went out for awhile this morning.
7. He said he likes you a whole lot more than me.
8. Let's talk while we walk.

9. Where did you lose your books?
10. Don't you see why we didn't keep your notes?
11. Who's going to help the other boy?
12. Whose black dog is that?

13. Whose white hat is there on the ground?
14. Who's sleeping in that old car?
15. Who's in front of that other line?
16. Whose child is crying?

It's been a very warm month here. We played a lot of games while it was nice out. The grass is just starting to get green. I'm glad that you're going to come see us for awhile.

After List 24

1. You're welcome to come with us!
2. This is the only world we have.
3. Their boys can't come over after work.
4. It became dark and cold that evening.

5. We can draw what we want to become.
6. They're playing house under the bed.
7. Who saw what these boys did this morning?
8. It is true if it's a fact.

9. It's the only one that's open!
10. Can't you just act like you're saying goodbye?
11. I love to work with others.
12. Whose words did I start to say?

13. These men have been around the whole world!
14. Can you tell me whether it's cold or hot?
15. We should stop over there for awhile.
16. Doesn't she have to work at some other place?

It's a fact that their child loves to draw. He's very good at it. He wants to be the best in the world. He only stops drawing when he sleeps or eats. He must get very good grades in art!

After List 25

1. They're going outside all by themselves today.
2. I don't understand why you put another check there.
3. They cannot come inside without her.
4. Maybe they'll forget which way you said to go.

5. We didn't understand why it stood there all by itself.
6. I walked into the room and looked around.
7. He never went by himself without telling us.
8. Maybe they're doing a whole lot more than that!

9. Could you put another hot dog on the *grill* outside?
10. Today is the second day of the month.
11. There are only seven days in a week.
12. Their house was about to start on fire!

13. You shouldn't cry when you're playing with them.
14. Your dog goes to sleep in front of my house every day.
15. Hasn't she asked herself whether it's true?
16. Maybe they aren't going to sleep there.

Once upon a time there were two blue boys. No one could tell which was which. They didn't like to talk about being blue. But they once said they wanted to be green!

Braden

After List 26

1. Thank you very much for your help.
2. The spring of the year should be nice and warm.
3. Come along with me for a nice long walk.
4. It was the same length as her arm.
5. I think I hear talking outside.
6. Bring that thing over here.
7. We did not hear you calling us.
8. Here is the dear child I told you about.
9. I think their house is on this street.
10. Do you live near here?
11. I love the strength of your big horse.
12. Has it been a long week for you?
13. I do not think this will be a clear morning.
14. Maybe I can become strong if I try.
15. Would you like to play outside among the trees?
16. Is this the second month of the year?
17. I forget whether they said yes or no.
18. Could you try to call back in about an hour?
19. That boy should come to the front of the room.
20. How have you been feeling this year?

After List 27

1. The teacher really wants to talk to you!
2. Please leave your books near my *desk*.
3. Should we go east or west from here?
4. We should at least say hello to him after we eat!
5. You will lose the game if you try to cheat.
6. It isn't easy to teach in the spring.
7. Can you reach around that thing?
8. You're welcome to speak to each of them.
9. What is its real strength?
10. My arm has been really weak for awhile.
11. Which teacher has been out sick all week?
12. Is that man weak or strong?
13. The street was filled with large white horses!
14. They're trying to work a whole lot more this week!
15. I think you're going to lose your place!
16. Why aren't those boys outside today?
17. Their teacher really likes facts!
18. At least we could ask which way is east!
19. Why shouldn't they go for a walk by themselves?
20. They're filling their car with books.

After List 28

1. The leader must have a good reason for doing that.
2. Please try not to scare the animals.
3. Don't you think spring is the best time of the year?
4. No, that's not what I meant at all!
5. Yes, I really care for my dear child.
6. No, they're not ready to start today.
7. Yes, two of the boys are really mean.
8. Yes, the sea was dark and cold that evening.
9. You must be in front to lead.
10. Please help us clean the street.
11. Didn't you read any of their books yet?
12. They will come just in case.
13. I meant to thank you for your nice gift when I saw you.
14. Maybe they're doing their work over there today.
15. You're not going to scare their leader!
16. Their horse goes up and down the street every morning.

Our team is not ready to start playing this season. Our leader thinks the reason is we're not trying as hard this year. We're not as strong as the other teams. At least we have fun even when we lose.

After List 29

1. Please put those two things down over there.
2. Is your house brown or green?
3. Our teacher doesn't allow us to cheat.
4. Why is this town so dirty?

5. The first girl in line began to talk.
6. Their leader has more power than ours does.
7. Which of these girls is in third grade?
8. The south part of town is clean.

9. When can we begin to eat?
10. How does a bird fly?
11. I want to meet you however we can.
12. Many of their girls are going away now.

13. Two of the girls are strong and four are weak.
14. They aren't going to work today.
15. We haven't been here for very long.
16. They couldn't hear the girl speak.

My first grade teacher was really nice. She helped me read so I was ready for second grade. I don't think I'll ever forget her. I wish I could thank her now.

After List 30

1. We're trying to choose a school for the girls.
2. Their food is not too good.
3. They're really not too strong.
4. It's too soon to see the moon.

5. Please close your left eye.
6. It's too soon to tell how he's feeling.
7. The bird is loose in their room!
8. These streets really aren't too smooth.

9. There is a bear on the loose!
10. My whole body feels weak and cold.
11. Could you send me a copy of your book?
12. What shall we wear today?

13. They're trying to choose the best food.
14. Whose dirty things are these?
15. Who's more than seven years old?
16. I can't bear to hear what you plan to wear!

Did you hear whether or not school will close this afternoon? The teacher said it will stay open. The third grade will go away for awhile, however. They'll allow us a day off next month.

After List 31

1. Do you know who's ready to go?
2. Throw that yellow ball to their dog.
3. Aren't you going to show me their notes?
4. Would you fix our window tomorrow?

5. You're trying to follow a man who's lost.
6. You've shown me more than I really want to see.
7. Doesn't she own the third house on the street?
8. They're going to grow up whether they want to or not.

9. They haven't known the two leaders for too long.
10. Please don't blow on your food to cool it.
11. He's too slow to be ready for the team.
12. Maybe they've got a really good reason!

13. They both said that it's too low to use.
14. Haven't the boys shown you where to find your room?
15. Their house is way too big for just two.
16. Why doesn't your second girl like school?

This afternoon I saw an animal sit down just below our window. It looked weak and dirty. It didn't have too much strength left. I felt bad when our dog ran over to scare it away.

After List 32

1. I can't stand too much more waiting!
2. I'm afraid it's going to rain again this afternoon.
3. The main reason they're paid well is that they work hard.
4. Do you know whether they're against us?

5. The air seems very cold near the sea.
6. You're not being fair with us!
7. I can't wait here by myself for too long.
8. Your hair doesn't look very dirty.

9. It's not too easy to raise animals.
10. You'll fail the test if you try to cheat.
11. The girl laid one thing after another on her desk.
12. Who's waiting to become the leader?

13. Maybe it's just plain food but it's very good!
14. I'm afraid he'll be too sick to work again tomorrow.
15. Haven't they paid for their rooms yet?
16. They're trying to bring up their child to say please and thank you.

Each of them said that their team would be the best of the year. It can't be true! Only one team can be first. Please tell me which team you think will reach the top.

After List 33

1. Once I knew quite a few of their names.
2. I don't believe I've ever seen such a nice view!
3. Do you hear the wind blowing outside?
4. The chief threw another piece of wood on the fire.

5. I'm afraid his heart isn't too strong.
6. The chief reason they lie is they're afraid.
7. Aren't you going to eat a piece of pie?
8. Doesn't he believe that they meant what they said?

9. It's too bad when you fail again after trying really hard.
10. She threw a *rock* at the bird to scare it away.
11. They're too weak to speak to their teacher.
12. Please leave that window open for awhile.

13. A few of the girls came from this street, too.
14. Thank you again for keeping your desk so clean.
15. I don't believe that what you're *saying* is true.
16. Whose piece of pie is this?

Our new horse died out in that large field. A strong wind blew a tree down and it fell on top of him. I wish he didn't have to die! I loved him and he would follow me around while I worked.

After List 34

1. We'd better find out when to go to dinner tomorrow.
2. The sea is supposed to be quiet this morning.
3. Didn't you hear what happened to their house?
4. Summer break came all of a sudden.

5. It doesn't really matter when we eat breakfast.
6. I don't suppose you understand why he's still waiting.
7. They haven't gotten away for a very long time.
8. They're too afraid of what could happen.

9. The view from the bottom is great!
10. The main reason we don't believe you is that we know how you lie!
11. Two of the boys threw down their books.
12. We could hear lots of birds outside.

13. Who's going to walk into that dark old house first?
14. Breakfast is supposed to be a quiet time of day.
15. Two really great things happened last summer!
16. They're too fair to throw away your piece of pie!

What happened here while I was gone? Didn't you know you're not supposed to break any windows? I'm afraid your mom will be really mad at you for throwing rocks. Why didn't you stop to think about it first?

After List 35

1. I slipped and fell as I stepped off the *stage*.
2. The animal was running and hopping all around.
3. They're getting ready to go sledding.
4. Their car will be stopping for us soon.

5. The rain hasn't stopped dropping from the trees yet.
6. We're planning to go swimming more than ever this summer.
7. I'm beginning to think we should have planned this better.
8. First he grabbed my hat and then he dropped it in the mud.

9. Why are we waiting again this afternoon?
10. It was very warm at the beginning of the summer.
11. There aren't too many teachers who want to play.
12. Oh, no! I dropped some of your things and they broke!

13. I can't wait too long for dinner.
14. Quit hopping around and clean your room!
15. Why are their hands getting so dirty each day?
16. Please stop running and be quiet for awhile!

I hear she's beginning to swim a few times each month. It's supposed to help her feel better at work. She's had too much to do and she's been working too hard. She'll be sick again if she doesn't start to rest more.

After List 36

1. We used to live in the green house down the street.
2. I'm really too scared to try doing that again!
3. They liked living near their school.
4. I was hoping you could have breakfast with us.

5. They're coming to see our new dining room tomorrow.
6. The moon is shining over the quiet sea.
7. Why are you using so many words to say goodbye?
8. They're too tired to go outside again today.

9. Thank you for giving me so much to believe in.
10. I suppose you're moving on after tomorrow.
11. Do you know why this is taking so long today?
12. They've lived here for at least two years.

13. Why are your girls so scared?
14. I used to believe what they told me was true.
15. They said just what they meant and I liked it!
16. Won't you two miss your teams while you're gone?

They're making plans to ride their horses tomorrow. The animals are kept in a field outside the next town. They'll be taking them for a good long run and then stopping to eat. I believe they'll be too tired to do much more after that!

After List 37

1. I'm afraid nobody will be waiting for us.
2. Nobody knows who's coming for dinner.
3. They're stopping for awhile anyway.
4. I don't understand why anybody would lie.

5. Somebody around here must know something!
6. Everyone is supposed to follow the leader.
7. Everything seemed a little dirty.
8. I saw birds flying everywhere I looked.

9. Sometimes I watch the same show again and again.
10. I think their house is somewhere along here.
11. We didn't catch too many fish this morning.
12. I need to stretch a little and then go for a walk.

13. Somebody said you knew who broke the window.
14. It's easy to fail but it's better to win.
15. Our clock isn't running too well.
16. Everyone is a little bit tired.

Sometimes it seems the same everywhere I go. I never hear anything new. Everyone says something bad about somebody. But nobody knows everything about anybody!

After List 38

1. Be careful to put everything right in the center of the room.
2. Yesterday was really wonderful.
3. I wonder if winter will come later this year.
4. Please cover that pan of water over in the corner.
5. The road was awful until yesterday.
6. What type of board do you need?
7. Something wonderful is supposed to happen later this afternoon.
8. Winter is a wonderful season if you like sledding.
9. They're planning to wait until their leader comes back.
10. Sometimes I wonder why nothing is ever easy.
11. You're among the first to understand what I mean.
12. They weren't going to watch us anyway.
13. Your heart is what keeps your whole body going.
14. We're beginning to wonder whether they're coming.
15. I'm afraid nobody has been stopping here this year.
16. Let's try to get to the bottom of this!

Take the main road going out of town. Go by the school and up the hill. Turn left at the first corner after the big field. Then keep going for six or seven miles until you see a little white house.

After List 39

1. It's so pleasant here early in the morning.
2. The weather has been very hot and dry.
3. I heard that their leader is dead!
4. We learned how to make bread in school today.
5. Could you please measure the water for the bread?
6. How heavy is the earth?
7. Everyone helped them search for their little dog.
8. We're beginning to learn something new about swimming.
9. Let's start living instead of thinking about death.
10. Its head is large but its eyes are little.
11. Nobody knows whether the weather will be good.
12. Let's go tomorrow instead of today.
13. He was hoping you wouldn't believe that little lie.
14. They're scared to death of the water.
15. The center line of the road should be yellow.
16. Doesn't he need to measure first?

We're used to being very careful about checking the weather. Once we planned a long trip and the rain was awful. We stopped trying to go swimming and just stayed inside. Now we watch and if it's going to be bad we leave on another day.

After List 40

1. They might die if they don't learn to fight.
2. The United States is a wonderful place to live.
3. We'd never want to live anywhere on earth but (your state)!
4. Maybe you're right to forget everything that happened there.
5. Mr. White said he goes running every night.
6. Ms. Green could just see her way by the light of the moon.
7. That cover is really tight!
8. They liked coming to see the United States of America.
9. The American flag was flying high over the school.
10. We'll have to buy everything in (your city) later.
11. Have you heard about the big fight?
12. There weren't many others around that morning.
13. Whose girls haven't been taking their food?
14. It's not easy to search at night.
15. We might buy everything right here.
16. What type of board do you want?

I wonder whether you know why the United States of America is such a wonderful place to live. It's true that our leaders might not be right about everything. But any American can work hard to make life better for himself. That isn't true in many other places on earth.

After List 41

1. We bought enough bread for the whole group.
2. I thought somebody was supposed to be waiting for us.
3. There weren't enough young men here until yesterday.
4. She brought something for everyone.

5. Ms. Brown walked for hours through the streets of (your city).
6. Don't touch anything that says it's private.
7. You're my best friend because we care about each other.
8. We stopped for awhile between the two towns.

9. They heard a little bit more yesterday, though.
10. It isn't too easy to seem that tough, though.
11. Who's coming over before breakfast?
12. It's great that the weather is so pleasant, though.

13. We're running away because we're scared to death!
14. This is a private note just between friends.
15. I thought they'd bought more than enough food before yesterday.
16. You should be careful not to touch anything that might break.

A group of tough young boys was outside trying to pick a fight. We told them to go away because we'd had enough. They wouldn't leave, though. Instead they started throwing rocks through the window.

After List 42

1. They're writing to the young man who taught fourth grade.
2. There's nothing wrong with the race course.
3. Don't laugh at my handwriting!
4. We knew there was something wrong when we heard about the wreck.

5. I heard laughter coming from the dining room.
6. The writer laughed at the joke I wrote.
7. We've written to everybody about the weather.
8. Why don't we let everyone in the group write to friends?

9. Somebody caught a big fish between here and the sea.
10. He might not be dead if he'd been more careful.
11. Yesterday we learned about the beginning of the earth.
12. Why weren't your friends searching for the wreck, too?

13. It's too early to measure everything you bought.
14. Laughter between friends is wonderful.
15. Be careful not to touch that awful thing until tomorrow.
16. I wonder whether they've caught anything new.

Mr. Brown taught a course in writing to the fourth grade. They wrote jokes to make their friends laugh. They wrote what they thought about school. They wrote thank you notes to everybody who helped them.

After List 43

1. Are you sure tomorrow will be Sunday?
2. They're planning to return next Thursday night.
3. Their girl was hurt on Tuesday afternoon.
4. What's the purpose of waiting until Friday?

5. You'll get your turn on Wednesday morning.
6. Saturday is a wonderful day to play.
7. The group went further today than they did last Monday.
8. We'll be sure to talk to you during the week.

9. They bought too much sugar yesterday.
10. Do you believe that it's right or wrong to be mean?
11. Wednesday will be the first day of the year.
12. I heard that the wreck happened early Thursday morning.

13. He dropped my lunch and then stepped on it on purpose.
14. Those boys threw something through the window last Tuesday.
15. They're not getting better because they're not trying very hard.
16. Let's go for a walk through the streets of (your city).

They're planning to leave before breakfast on Wednesday morning. Thursday they're stopping to go swimming in the sea. On Friday they'll go further to see the sugar fields. They will return by Saturday night for sure.

After List 44

1. Please draw a single circle in the middle of your paper.
2. Remember that you'll get in trouble if you fight.
3. I was really surprised to hear about their terrible wreck!
4. People are too important to hurt on purpose.

5. Chocolate is their favorite snack.
6. What a pleasant surprise!
7. What's the problem with this program?
8. I promise I'll write to you before we leave (your city).

9. I was surprised to learn that Wednesday is their favorite day.
10. You'll get in terrible trouble if you touch that chocolate!
11. Remember that it's wrong to laugh at people who are having trouble.
12. Our program will be the best in the whole world!

13. Let's stretch this thing down the middle of the road.
14. I believe you've gotten even further than you thought.
15. I promise you I'll remember to bring a surprise!
16. All the trouble started last Saturday!

It's important to remember every promise you make to people. A friend might have hurt feelings if you forget even a single promise. It's better to surprise someone than to make a promise and then not keep it. Be careful because you don't want to make trouble for others.

After List 45

1. We gave some bread to the family because they were hungry.
2. You're so lucky to live out in the country!
3. I'd be happy to study with you after dinner.
4. This is a pretty busy city!

5. I'm sorry I didn't remember to carry your books.
6. Your enemy isn't too happy that you're so tough.
7. Please hurry because the program is just beginning.
8. Their little girl is really a beauty!

9. Remember that this story is quite important.
10. Your friend is lucky to have such great handwriting.
11. Their family has come through many hard times.
12. It's so heavy that I'm not sure I can carry it.

13. We've been so busy that we haven't had enough time for people.
14. This country field is my favorite place to study.
15. We're sorry we have to hurry away so early.
16. I was surprised to see them so happy after all the trouble.

It's not easy to study in our dining room. Everyone in the family is busy and I get hungry when I smell dinner. It's pretty hard to think and learn. It's better to study in my private room.

After List 46

1. That student is almost always alone.
2. We won't be having recess unless everyone can be quiet.
3. They're already studying for their written test on Wednesday.
4. I took a long lonely walk through the busy city.

5. Who's hurrying across the room?
6. I thought you might want their address.
7. We'll have another writing lesson on Thursday.
8. I heard some terrible things about your enemy yesterday.

9. Although she knows them, she doesn't remember their address.
10. Although we're hurrying, we'll be a little late.
11. Although we're carrying your surprise, we can't show it to you.
12. Although he's almost always alone, he isn't lonely.

13. We shouldn't go much further across this lonely country.
14. They're studying the wrong lesson!
15. I can't believe how much beauty there is on this earth!
16. Don't call unless you're stopping early.

It seems like they're almost always hurrying. Maybe it's because they're too busy to remember what life is about. Although they're lucky to be working, they don't have enough time for their friends and family. Taking time for people is very important.

After List 47

1. Almost everyone cries when they've been hurt.
2. We tried to surprise the writing teacher.
3. They hurried to get here because they wanted to hear your stories.
4. This is a beautiful place to have a business!
5. Luckily we're earlier than we thought.
6. Which group is the easiest to teach?
7. They took a trip through many countries around the world.
8. Clean things are prettier than dirty ones.

9. We studied about the terrible things their enemies did.
10. Their families really understand what happiness means.
11. I meant to tell you about the beautiful view!
12. We should be studying instead of playing.

13. Which countries were your favorites?
14. The purpose of going to school is to learn.
15. I'm not sure why all these animals are dead.
16. It's prettier outside during the early morning hours.

We tried to tell true stories to our families instead of telling lies. But they still couldn't believe the terrible things that had happened during the night. We were so scared that we hurried home earlier than ever before. Our families said we were pretty lucky to get away from the trouble in time.

After List 48

1. No person on earth is perfect.
2. He couldn't bear the idea of going to prison.
3. Nobody else wants to practice until next period.
4. Perhaps you didn't notice that the office is across the street.
5. The noise last Wednesday was terrible.
6. Please point to the person with the noisy laughter.
7. Her voice was like poison.
8. Did you notice that beautiful bird?
9. This is a perfect way for almost anybody to learn.
10. I'm sorry to tell you that everything else was their idea.

After List 49

1. The captain is only twenty-one years old.
2. I heard they think it's forty million years old.
3. Are these your favorite clothes?
4. That mountain is supposed to be nineteen thousand feet high.
5. He's certainly at least ninety years old.
6. Perhaps eleven or twelve of the young men are already hungry.
7. I'm certain that someone will entertain the people while they wait.
8. Once upon a time the enemy tried to poison our water.
9. More than a hundred people were there in the office.
10. They've written to the captain at least twenty-two times.

After List 50

1. Your sister is really beautiful!
2. My parents notice everything.
3. Are your aunt and uncle in the dining room yet?
4. Her cousin has a son who's studying writing.
5. I haven't seen my niece and nephew for twelve years.
6. Is your grandfather really a hundred years old?
7. Grandma is my favorite relative.
8. They have two daughters and eleven sons.
9. Their mother and father are almost perfect parents.
10. Luckily his brother isn't too noisy.

After List 51

1. The teacher on recess duty must know the rules.
2. Let's be careful not to tell anybody our secret.
3. The secretary used to live out on the prairie.
4. I love the beautiful northern lakes and forests.
5. You can't enjoy something if you destroy it.
6. Could you wait outside for a minute or two?
7. This is the most modern hospital in the city.
8. The circles made a beautiful pattern.
9. Perhaps it will be easier to talk together if we're alone.
10. I can fix these stairs if you have some new boards.

After List 52

1. The library will be closed during December.
2. The summer months are June, July and August.
3. Remember how beautiful it was last March.
4. The trouble started between January and April.
5. My grandma was born on May 3, 1938.
6. Saturday will be the first of February already!
7. October is her favorite month of the year.
8. They really learned a lot during September.
9. Everything was all right when we left in November.
10. America was born on July 4, 1776.

After List 53

1. I doubt that their answer will surprise you.
2. Please fasten your climbing ropes together.
3. If you're careful to listen to the next sentence, you'll know what she means.
4. He only took half of the medicine for his blood.
5. Everyone climbed the mountain.
6. We listened but we couldn't hear anything.
7. We saw a lot of poor and hungry families in the country.
8. What's the central idea of her book?
9. It's hard for my grandma to climb the stairs.
10. I doubt the hospital has enough medicine for everyone.

After List 54

1. I got a terrible stomach ache after dinner.
2. It was a tragedy when that car went off the edge of the bridge.
3. It's impossible to know her true character.
4. Somebody's climbing up the ridge.
5. You can't force people to want knowledge.
6. We might be able to make a simple table.
7. This article says almost anything is possible.
8. The captain often listened to the birds sing.
9. Don't climb around under the bridge!
10. Who's your favorite character?

After List 55

1. We barely got the children to safety in time.
2. I sincerely hope this isn't your final statement!
3. The women are especially tired.
4. He's writing to one very special woman!
5. We're studying the arctic in our social studies class.
6. They don't ask much since they learned how to listen.
7. We finally moved into the new library in February.
8. No one can argue with his last statement.
9. The teacher was especially careful to listen to her students.
10. The children are sincerely sorry about what happened.

After List 56

1. Several women are walking toward that building.
2. I guess the guard is guilty of taking the money.
3. There's a sign on the island which says climbing there isn't safe.
4. They're probably beginning to build their house already.
5. I was surprised that no one there knew our language.
6. The new library was built early in August.
7. I like recess, lunch, etc.
8. Doesn't the guard have a key to the other building?
9. It's probably impossible to have too much knowledge.
10. I guess several of them will go to prison because they're guilty.

After List 57

1. Why were you absent from gym yesterday?
2. He's skiing straight down the mountain.
3. I passed that building on my bicycle last night.
4. This author writes truly interesting books.
5. You'd better tie your shoes.
6. He doesn't seem to have much interest in buying your motor.
7. The doctor doesn't want to get into an argument with you!
8. They're tying those guard dogs to a post.
9. Luckily he has a lot of interest in the family business.
10. We passed towns, fields, mountains, etc.

After List 58

1. This picture doesn't make any sense!
2. The author didn't have more than a nickel in his pocket.
3. Pay attention to your regular doctor!
4. Come buy a ticket for just a dollar.
5. This addition problem is easy to figure.
6. Action is more important than speech.
7. What direction is the library building?
8. There's probably a good answer to that question.
9. We finally found a calendar for February.
10. I guess they've been going the wrong direction since Wednesday.

After List 59

1. Do you really expect me to accept that excuse?
2. This is an example of the development of government.
3. I can't explain your experience.
4. Walking is excellent exercise.
5. I liked everything in the show except the tragedy.
6. This is an exciting example of what doctors can do.
7. The children are finally showing some excitement.
8. Be careful not to excite the guards.
9. Some people expect the government to figure out answers to all their problems.
10. Excuse me but I can probably explain.

After List 60

1. They're definitely planning to come tomorrow.
2. This road is completely straight for miles.
3. We're extremely interested in your ideas.
4. Practically everyone expects life to be exciting.
5. Their statement is actually quite complete.
6. Experience is usually the best teacher.
7. Their interest was definite and immediate.
8. Generally we do things the usual way.
9. It's not practical to do this immediately.
10. The actual argument was carefully developed.

After List 61

1. It wasn't convenient to check a reference book.
2. The existence of lightning is especially interesting.
3. It's my opinion that your patient is quite intelligent.
4. What's the difference between speech and language?
5. This type of music is a lot different than what I'm used to.
6. The United States is an independent country.
7. Be careful that you don't misspell any words.
8. This magazine talks about the benefits of independence.
9. A teacher must be extremely patient, intelligent, etc.
10. My daughter has quite a different opinion.

After List 62

1. Neither of my two neighbors is patient.
2. That music has a foreign rhythm.
3. They had to seize eight of the receipts.
4. Don't try to deceive the doctor.
5. Didn't you receive either of the pictures?
6. What's the height of that building?
7. We definitely thought something was weird.
8. We're studying grammar in our language class.
9. The doctor needs to know your height and weight.
10. My neighbors seem to have a lot of leisure time.

After List 63

1. I guarantee you that this incident was an accident.
2. It's getting more and more difficult to escape.
3. Sometimes you're responsible whether you're guilty or innocent.
4. They accidentally accepted too much money.
5. This procedure is similar to others you already understand.
6. Which particular poem is your favorite?
7. We asked for separate checks at the restaurant.
8. The accident was similar to another tragedy which happened last February.
9. We can't guarantee that you'll have separate rooms.
10. They're extremely scared of getting that particular disease.

After List 64

1. I suggest that we concentrate on education.
2. It's difficult to imagine what effect this will have.
3. Could you repeat your description?
4. Sometimes you can identify people by their pronunciation.
5. Repetition can be a good way to learn some things.
6. The weight you're carrying will affect your speed.
7. Could you please describe the people who escaped?
8. Prepare to continue immediately.
9. Knowledge and education aren't our biggest national problems.
10. Would you please repeat the pronunciation?

After List 65

1. I recommend that you appear before the committee on Wednesday.
2. We don't want to embarrass or disappoint you.
3. It isn't necessary for the lines to be parallel.
4. Be careful as you approach this special opportunity.
5. How fast can you make a sandwich disappear?
6. This system will accommodate many different procedures.
7. You'll definitely seem weird if you exaggerate too much.
8. Will this room accommodate the whole committee?
9. I suggest that we go in the opposite direction.
10. It will embarrass him if his keys disappear again.

After List 66

1. It's definitely a privilege to go to college.
2. This machine is difficult to control.
3. They're equipped to handle almost any occurrence.
4. His journal referred to an area near the college.
5. Something weird seems to be occurring.
6. He's hoping to get some relief soon!
7. You can achieve many things if you commit yourself.
8. The accident occurred near the old bridge.
9. Independence is a privilege.
10. Nobody knows what will occur tomorrow.

After List 67

1. I apologize that I didn't recognize you.
2. Let me acquaint you with a friend of mine.
3. Her feelings were hurt because of the criticism.
4. I didn't realize that you lived such a long distance from the city.
5. They can't perform well if all you do is criticize them.
6. Your summary is brilliant!
7. Its appearance was very peculiar.
8. I hope your acquaintance will accept my apology.
9. There's something familiar about this restaurant.
10. You realize that he'll probably recognize us!

After List 68

1. The principal wants to discuss your decision.
2. He had a lot of success in his profession.
3. Physical education class will not be in the gym tomorrow.
4. Are they making any progress with their discussion?
5. You can't easily succeed unless you decide what's most important.
6. What's the big occasion?
7. That character doesn't possess anything in particular.
8. The professor decided to teach the principles of government.
9. Do you recognize the principal?
10. The committee decided to discuss the criticism.

After List 69

1. Those mischievous boys need some discipline!
2. I want to apologize because I have a guilty conscience.
3. The professor tells a lot of serious stories.
4. The next scene will fascinate you.
5. It's a privilege to have such a delicious dinner with you.
6. Their arguments are continuous.
7. I really appreciate your humorous approach.
8. They're nervous because their professor isn't conscious.
9. You'll need your scissors for science this morning.
10. Are you jealous of his success?

LETTER FORM

A **letter** is a written message addressed to a person or organization and most often sent through the **postal system**. There are two types of letters: friendly letters and business letters.

	Friendly Letter	*Business Letter*
Sent to	Friends Relatives Pen Pals	Companies Editors Government officials
Purpose	Keep in touch Make friends (pen pals) Say thank you Offer congratulations Apologize Send birthday or holiday greetings	Express an opinion Make a complaint Praise something good Ask for information Request materials Order a product
Writing	Usually handwritten.	Usually typed.
Return address	Sometimes is not included.	Often is part of printed letterhead stationery.
Date	May be abbreviated.	Never abbreviated.
Inside address	Never included.	Always included. Use the exact address that will be on the envelope.
Greeting	Follow with a comma (,). Normally use the person's first name.	Follow with a colon (:). Use a person's title and last name. If unknown, use *Dear Sir or Madam:* or *To Whom It May Concern:*
Body	Indent the first line of each paragraph.	Skip lines between paragraphs. Paragraphs may or may not be indented.
Closing	*Your friend,* *Love,* *Yours truly,*	*Sincerely,* *Sincerely yours,*
Signature	Sign with first name only, or first and last name.	Always sign in ink with both first and last names.
Typed name	Not included.	Always included in typewritten business letters. Usually, it is four spaces below the closing.

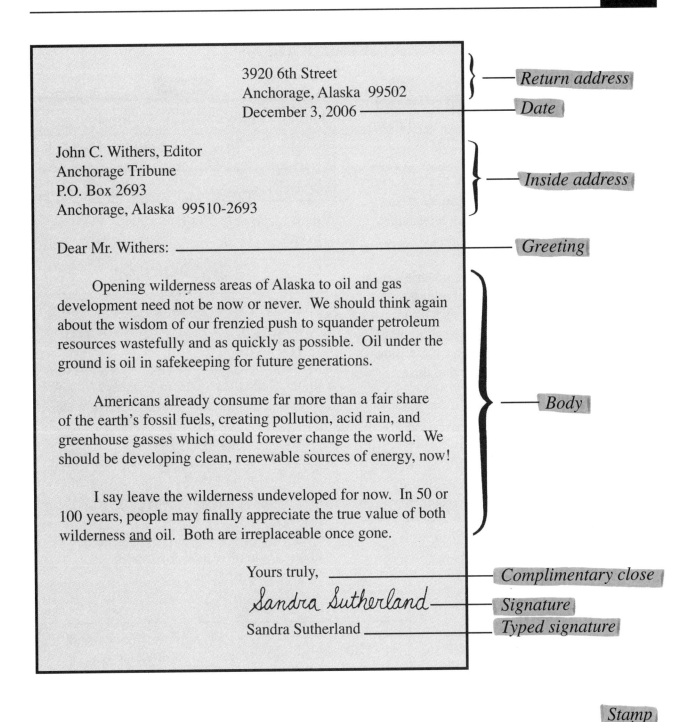

3920 6th Street
Anchorage, Alaska 99502
December 3, 2006 — **Return address**, **Date**

John C. Withers, Editor
Anchorage Tribune
P.O. Box 2693
Anchorage, Alaska 99510-2693 — **Inside address**

Dear Mr. Withers: — **Greeting**

Opening wilderness areas of Alaska to oil and gas development need not be now or never. We should think again about the wisdom of our frenzied push to squander petroleum resources wastefully and as quickly as possible. Oil under the ground is oil in safekeeping for future generations.

Americans already consume far more than a fair share of the earth's fossil fuels, creating pollution, acid rain, and greenhouse gasses which could forever change the world. We should be developing clean, renewable sources of energy, now!

I say leave the wilderness undeveloped for now. In 50 or 100 years, people may finally appreciate the true value of both wilderness <u>and</u> oil. Both are irreplaceable once gone. — **Body**

Yours truly, — **Complimentary close**

Sandra Sutherland — **Signature**
Sandra Sutherland — **Typed signature**

Stamp

Addressing an Envelope

Always include a zip code in the address and return address. Zip codes, first used in 1963, speed the sorting of mail. Nine digit zip codes were first used in 1981.

Return address
Sandra Sutherland
3920 6th Street
Anchorage, Alaska 99502

Address
John C. Withers, Editor
Anchorage Tribune
P.O. Box 2693
Anchorage, Alaska 99510-2693

BIBLIOGRAPHIC FORM

A **bibliography** is a list of books and other materials on a specific subject that have been used by a writer. When doing a research report, it is important to keep track of sources of information by recording the author, title, place of publication, name of publisher, and copyright date of each source. The bibliography, or list of sources, should be alphabetized and placed at the end of the report.

Different types of reference materials have slightly different punctuation and bibliographic form. If a piece of information, such as an author's name, is not available, leave it out and go to the next piece of information. If writing by hand, use underlines in place of italics.

Web Site

Anthony, Susan C. "Writing Samples and Ideas." *Susan C. Anthony.* 3 Jan 2007. < http://www.susancanthony.com/Resources/writing/writs.html>

Author. "Title of Article." *Title of web site.* Publication date. Producer or sponsor of site. Access date. <URL>

Book

Duvall, Betty. *Writing Right: A Guide to Improving Handwriting.* Spokane, WA: Ten Speed Press, 1979.

Author. *Title.* Place of Publication: Publisher, Date.

Magazine Article

Quateroni, Bob. "Awful Handwriting." *Saturday Evening Post* 265 (May 1993): 16.

Author. "Title of Article." *Periodical Name* Volume (Month and Year): Page Number.

Encyclopedia

Little Soldier, Lee M. "Handwriting." *The World Book Encyclopedia.* 2007.

Author. "Title of Article." *Name of Encyclopedia.* Date.

OUTLINE FORM

Roman numerals:

I = 1	**L** = 50	**M** = 1000
V = 5	**C** = 100	
X = 10	**D** = 500	

Add the values for the symbols from left to right: **XVII** = 10+5+1+1 = 17 When a smaller number is written to the *left* of a larger number, subtract the smaller number from the larger one just to its right, then add the result as usual: **IV** (1 before 5) = 5–1 = 4

Title of Outline	Poisonous Snakes of the United States

I. Main Heading
    A. Subheading
        1. Detail
            a. Sub-detail
            b. Sub-detail
        2. Detail
    B. Subheading
    C. Subheading
II. Main Heading
    A. Subheading
    B. Subheading
	I. Pit vipers
	    A. Rattlesnake
	        1. Characteristics
	            a. Size
	            b. Rattle
	        2. Range
	    B. Water moccasin
	    C. Copperhead
	II. Coral snakes
	    A. Eastern coral snake
	    B. Western coral snake

CAPITALIZATION

In this section, I've collected a resource bank of regularly-spelled titles and proper nouns that may be included in dictation sentences when the teacher decides to introduce or review a particular capitalization rule or objective. The words included are either on the 1000 word list or are in regular patterns taught in *Spelling Plus*. They are not organized in order of difficulty, so select what you use carefully.

All titles are of actual books, songs, paintings, etc. All place names are real. Consider challenging students to find out more about the titles or places mentioned in dictation sentences using an atlas, encyclopedia, or almanac.

Headline style capitalization, used in titles, should be taught. Not every word should be capitalized. The following guidelines are from the *Chicago Manual of Style*.

Capitalize:

1. The first word in a title.
2. The last word in a title.
3. All nouns, pronouns, adjectives, verbs and adverbs.
4. Subordinating conjunctions. See list on this page.

Do not capitalize (unless used as the first or last word of a title):

1. Articles: *a, an, the*.
2. Coordinating conjunctions. See list on this page.
3. Prepositions, regardless of length. See list on this page.
4. The infinitive *to*.

Subordinating Conjunctions (*capitalize*):

after	before	so	unless
although	if	that	whether
because	once	though	while

Coordinating Conjunctions (*don't capitalize*):

and	either	nor	or
but	neither	plus	yet

Prepositions (*do not capitalize*):

about	beside	like*	than*
above	besides	near	through
across	between	next	throughout
after	beyond	of	to
against	but	off	toward
along	by	on	towards
among	down	onto	under
around	during	out	unlike
as*	except	outside	until*
at	for*	over	up
before	from	past	upon
behind	in	per	with
below	inside	plus	within
beneath	into	since*	without

*These words may be used as either subordinating conjunctions, which should be capitalized, or prepositions, which should not. Since a good knowledge of grammar is required in order to tell the difference, they are listed here only as prepositions.

Challenge students to memorize postal abbreviations for the states before introducing capitalization of cities and towns (p. 52). When you dictate the state names, especially in a letter, they may write the abbreviation instead. Students should also memorize abbreviations for *street, avenue*, etc. which are on p. 46. You may wish to introduce a few common abbreviations a week from the list on p. 52.

Capitalize titles of books.

6 The Cat in the Hat
14 Gone with the Wind
14 One Fine Day
15 A Tree Is Nice
18 The Book of Three
18 Farmer Boy
18 The Horse and His Boy
18 The Whipping Boy
19 The Call of the Wild (Jack London)
23 By the Shores of Silver Lake
24 War of the Worlds
26 King of the Wind
26 On the Banks of Plum Creek
26 They Were Strong and Good

26 Where the Wild Things Are
27 Number the Stars
29 The First Four Years
29 The Girl Who Loved Wild Horses
31 The Big Snow
31 The Snowy Day
33 Brave New World
33 Heart of Darkness
35 The Biggest Bear
36 The Giving Tree
37 Little House in the Big Woods
38 The Long Winter
38 Up a Road Slowly
39 The Good Earth

40 The High King
41 May I Bring a Friend?
41 Through the Looking Glass
43 The Return of the King
45 These Happy Golden Years
46 Always Room for One More
47 Just So Stories
49 My Side of the Mountain
51 All Quiet on the Western Front
51 Little House on the Prairie
51 Little Town on the Prairie
55 The Funny Little Woman
55 Little Women
56 Treasure Island

Capitalize names of magazines.

6 U.S. Kids
9 Jack and Jill
12 Life
16 Car and Driver
16 Your Big Backyard
18 Boys' Life
18 Redbook
18 Time
19 Flying

24 Contact
28 Weekly Reader
29 Owl
33 Newsweek
33 U.S. News and World
    Report
34 Better Homes and
    Gardens
34 Ranger Rick

36 Racing for Kids
40 American Girl
41 Stone Soup
44 People
45 Country Home
45 Country Living
45 Family Circle
45 Kid City
47 Business Week

49 Seventeen
51 Southern Living
53 Outdoor Life
55 Highlights for Children
55 New Woman
56 Money
62 Weight Watchers
63 TV Guide
69 Super Science

Capitalize names of newspapers.

25 USA Today
27 West Palm Beach Post

33 New York Post
33 New York Times

38 Denver Post
49 Rocky Mountain News

66 Wall Street Journal

Capitalize titles of stories.

The Wind and the Sun
The Smile
The Time of Going Away
A Good Man Is Hard to
    Find
The Red Shoes
The White Cat
The Shadow

The Fox and the Crow
The Day It Rained Forever
Heart of the West
All Summer in a Day
The Snow Queen
The Little Red Hen
Two of Everything
The Golden Touch

The Garden Party
The Story of Live Dolls
Sleeping Beauty
The Story of the Three
    Bears
The Story of the Three
    Little Pigs

The Fire on the Mountain
The King of the Mountains
The Story of a Mother
The Twelve Brothers
The House That Jack Built
Men of Different Colors

Capitalize titles of chapters.

Capitalize titles of articles.

Note: Unalphabetized lists are in general order of spelling difficulty. The numbers refer to related *Spelling Plus* lists.

Capitalize titles of poems.

8 Grass (Carl Sandburg)
12 Fire and Ice (Robert Frost)
13 Days (Ralph Waldo Emerson)
15 Trees (Joyce Kilmer)
17 To a Mouse (Robert Burns)
26 Song of Myself (Walt Whitman)
31 The Snow Man (Wallace Stevens)

31 The Cross of Snow (Henry
   Wadsworth Longfellow)
33 The Far Field (Theodore
   Roethke)
34 The Raven (Edgar Allen Poe)
35 Stopping By Woods on a
   Snowy Evening (Robert Frost)

38 I Wonder as I Wander (Langston
   Hughes)
39 Death Be Not Proud (John Donne)
39 I Heard a Fly Buzz (Emily
   Dickinson)
54 The Bridge (Hart Crane)
59 Little Exercise (Elizabeth Bishop)

Capitalize titles of plays.

7 Bus Stop (William Inge, American)
11 The Waste Land (T.S. Eliot, British,
   1922)
12 As You Like It (Shakespeare,
   British)
14 All for Love (John Dryden, British,
   1677)
17 The Storm (Alexander Ostrovsky,
   Russian, 1860)
20 The Wild Duck (Henrik Ibsen,
   Norwegian, 1884)
21 Once in a Lifetime (Hart &
   Kaufman, 1930)

22 All's Well That Ends Well
   (Shakespeare, British)
22 You Can't Take It with You (Hart
   & Kaufman, 1937)
24 The Way of the World (William
   Congreve, British, 1700)
28 The Sea Gull (Anton Chekhov,
   Russian, 1896)
34 The Man Who Came to Dinner
   (Moss Hart & Geo. Kaufman,
   Americans, 1939)
45 A Month in the Country (Ivan
   Turgenev, Russian, 1850)

45 My Fair Lady
50 The Three Sisters (Anton
   Chekhov, Russian, 1901)
51 The Dark at the Top of the Stairs
   (William Inge, American)
55 What Every Woman Knows
   (James M. Barrie, British, 1908)
69 The Conscious Lovers (Sir
   Richard Steele, British, 1722)

Capitalize titles of television shows.

4 Batman
9 Still Standing
12 Dateline NBC
12 Prime Time Live
13 This Is Your Day
14 Day One
14 One Life to Live
15 Meet the Press
15 Wall Street Week
17 This Old House
18 CBS This Morning
22 I'll Fly Away

23 Who's the Boss?
24 Grace under Fire
24 Starting Over
26 Yes, Dear
28 Cold Case
28 Wild about Animals
30 Eye to Eye
30 Hard Copy
31 The Home Show
31 The Red Green Show
33 The View
33 World News Now

38 The Road Home
38 The Wonder Years
39 The Early Show
40 Good Morning
America
40 In the Heat of the Night
40 Nightline
40 The Price Is Right
40 The Tonight Show
41 Friends
43 As the World Turns
43 Saturday Night Live

44 People's Court
45 Family Matters
45 Spin City
47 Bold and the Beautiful
48 Less than Perfect
48 The Practice
51 60 Minutes
53 Two and a Half Men
55 All My Children
56 For Love or Money
62 Eight Simple Rules
64 Face the Nation

Capitalize titles of movies.

4 Batman
7 Top Gun
12 Nine to Five
14 Gone with the Wind
16 Star Wars
20 On Golden Pond

24 Jaws
28 The Dream Team
29 Working Girl
30 The Bear
32 Black Rain
32 Rain Man

33 Places in the Heart
38 Superman
39 The Learning Tree
40 Coming to America
40 High Noon

45 Three Men and a Baby
46 Always
47 Big Business
53 The Great Outdoors
61 The Sound of Music

Note: Lists are in general order of spelling difficulty. The numbers refer to related *Spelling Plus* lists.

Capitalize titles of songs.

8 This Land is Your Land
9 Deck the Halls
10 Let It Be
10 The Fox
11 Rock of Ages
12 You Are My Sunshine
14 The Rose
17 The Horses Run Around
18 In the Evening
20 My Good Old Man
20 Old Blue
20 Three Blind Mice
23 Tell Me Why
23 What Child Is This?
24 It's a Small World

24 Joy to the World
24 Top of the World
25 Today
26 Do You Hear What I Hear?
26 Four Strong Winds
26 God Save the King
28 Careless Love
29 Both Sides Now
29 Where Have All the Flowers Gone?
31 Blow the Man Down
31 Follow Me
31 Sweet and Low
31 Throw It Out the Window

34 Home on the Range
34 Morning Has Broken
34 The Hammer Song
37 Little Brown Jug
38 Cool Water
38 Deep River
38 One More River to Cross
39 Early Morning Rain
40 America
40 God Bless America
40 It Came Upon the Midnight Clear
40 Silent Night

44 Nobody Knows the Trouble I've Seen
45 Country Roads
45 Down in the Valley
45 Red River Valley
48 Big Rock Candy Mountain
49 Five Hundred Miles
49 Go Tell It On the Mountain
50 Grandfather's Clock
53 Poor Boy
55 The Midnight Special
56 That's Where My Money Goes

Capitalize titles of paintings or other works of art.

8 The Clockmaker (French, 1900)
20 The Golden Wall (1961)
26 The Swing (French, 1768)
28 The Gulf Stream (Winslow Homer, American, 1899)
29 Birthday (Russian, 1915)
30 Mona Lisa (Italian, 1503)
34 The Last Supper (Italian, 1495)

40 Nighthawks (Edward Hopper, American, 1940)
40 The Night Watch (Dutch, 1642)
42 The Shipwreck (J.M.W. Turner, British, 1805)
43 Return of the Hunters (1565)
45 The Starry Night (Vincent Van Gogh, Dutch)

50 Mother and Child (Pablo Picasso, Spanish, 1921)
55 Three Women (French, 1921)
55 Young Woman with a Water Jug (1660)
57 The Last Judgment (Michelangelo, Italian)

Capitalize titles used to refer to people.

Mr.	Miss	Captain	King	Prince	Professor	President	Jr.*
Ms.	Dr.	General	Queen	Princess	Pope	Senator	Sr.*
Mrs.	Rev.	Governor					

*Sr. (Senior) and Jr. (Junior) are used when father and son have the same name. John H. Green Sr.

Capitalize names of people (first names).

Al	Bruce	Hal	Jess	Larry	Nick	Robby	Tim
Amy	Chris	Hank	Jill	Mark	Norm	Ron	Tina
Andy	Dale	Harry	Jim	Mary	Pam	Rose	Tom
Ann(e)	Dan	Jack	Joe	May	Pat	Roy	Tony
Barb	Deb	Jake	John	Meg	Paul	Russ	Val
Barry	Denny	James	Joy	Micky	Peggy	Sal	Van
Becky	Dick	Jan	Judy	Mike	Penny	Sally	Vicky
Ben	Ed	Jane	June	Milt	Pete	Sam	Walt
Bess	Fay(e)	Jay	Kay(e)	Molly	Polly	Sid	Wanda
Betty	Frank	Jed	Ken	Nan	Ray	Tad	
Bill	Fred	Jeff	Kim	Nat	Rick	Tammy	
Bob	George	Jenny	Kitty	Ned	Rob	Ted	

Note: Unalphabetized lists are in general order of spelling difficulty. The numbers refer to related *Spelling Plus* lists.

Capitalize initials: A. L. Smith

Capitalize names of people (surnames).

Armstrong	Chung	Frost	Jackson	Newman	Rust	Swanson	Voss
Banks	Clark	Gates	James	Newton	Sam	Sweet	Wade
Beck	Cook	Goodman	Johnson	Page	Sanchez	Swift	Walker
Becker	Cousins	Goodrich	Jones	Park	Sands	Taft	Walls
Bell	Cox	Gore	Kent	Parker	Shell	Tanner	Wang
Best	Crook	Grant	Kim	Parks	Short	Tate	Ward
Black	Cross	Graves	King	Peck	Skinner	Thacker	Waters
Blackwell	Dale	Gray	Kirk	Pope	Small	Tong	Watson
Blake	Day	Green	Lake	Price	Smart	Tope	Weeks
Bock	Dow	Hall	Lane	Prince	Smith	Tower	Wellman
Bond	Downs	Ham	Lee	Rand	Snow	Townsend	Wells
Bridges	Drake	Harding	Long	Ray	Sparks	Trent	West
Brink	Drew	Hess	Love	Rice	Springer	Trotter	Westover
Brooks	Duke	Hicks	Luke	Rich	Stark	Troy	White
Brown	Fink	Hill	Mack	Rivers	Storm	Trueblood	Winter
Burns	Fish	Holt	Marsh	Rockwell	Stone	Tucker	Wong
Bush	Flint	Hood	May	Rose	Stout	Turner	Woods
Chang	Ford	Horn	Mills	Ross	Strand	Underhill	Yang
Chapman	Fox	Huff	Moon	Roy	Strang	Underwood	York
Chase	Freeman	Hunt	Moss	Rush	Strong	Vance	Young
Chong	French	Hunter	Nash	Russ	Street	Vest	Zick

Capitalize names of pets.

Bear	Buffy	Frisky	Nip	Ranger	Shadow	Snuggles	Whiskers
Beauty	Buster	Jet	Pike	Ringo	Silver	Spike	Windy
Bingo	Comet	Midnight	Pluto	Rocky	Skippy	Spot	Wolf
Boomer	Duke	Mista	Prince	Rover	Snapper	Star	
Buck	Dusty	Misty	Puff	Ruby	Snoopy	Tip	
Buddy	Fluffy	Muffy	Rainbow	Rusty	Snowy	Tuck	

Capitalize nationalities and languages.

Arabic	English	German	Hebrew	Italian	Polish	Russian	Swedish
Dutch	French	Greek	Irish	Latin	Roman	Spanish	Welsh

Capitalize names of religions.

Buddhist	Catholic	Christian	Jewish	Muslim	Quaker

Capitalize names of political groups.

Democrat	Republican	Independent	Green Party	Whigs

Capitalize names of groups, organizations, clubs, businesses.

Students should know the abbreviation for Association (Assn.).

YMCA
YWCA
Camp Fire
Blue Cross
Boy Scouts
World Wildlife Fund
PTA (Parent Teacher Assn.)
The Fund for Animals
Girl Scouts
American Camping Assn.
American Lung Assn.
American Red Cross
Bank of America
Boys' Clubs of America
Sports Car Club of America

United Way of America
Friends of the Earth
United States Post Office
American War Mothers
American Library Assn.
March of Dimes
Indoor Sports Club
National Guard
American Hospital Assn.
Country Music Assn.
National Restaurant Assn.
National Basketball Assn.
National Business Education Assn.
National Press Club
United Nations

American Council for the Arts
American Council on Education
American Horse Council
Children's Book Council
Council of State Governments
National Council of Teachers of English
National Council of Women
National Council on Death and Dying
National Home Study Council
National Music Council
National Safety Council
National Science Teachers Assn.
Student Council

Capitalize names of continents.

North America   South America   Europe   Asia   Africa   Australia   Antarctica

Capitalize names of countries.

Australia	Chad	Denmark	France	India	Mexico	Spain
Brazil	China	England	Germany	Italy	Norway	Turkey
Canada	Congo	Finland	Iceland	Japan	South Africa	United States

Capitalize names of geographical regions (not directions).

Central America   Deep South   Far East   Middle East   New England   Southeast Asia

Capitalize names of states and provinces.

These state names are relatively easy to spell. Students should learn state postal abbreviations. See p. 50.

| Alaska | Idaho | Maryland | New Mexico | Ohio | Vermont |
| Colorado | Maine | Montana | New York | Texas | Washington |

Capitalize names of cities and towns.

These cities and towns are in the states listed above. Others are on the following page.

Alaska	Colorado	Maryland	Montana	New Mexico	New York	Ohio	Texas
Flat	Brush	Rock Hall	Big Sky	Black Rock	Cold Springs	Black Horse	Midland
Nome	Grand Lake	Camp Springs	Three Forks	Shiprock	East Hills	North Bend	Lone Star
May Creek	Loveland	Chase	Hot Springs	Red River	White Plains	Forest Hills	Round Rock
Central	South Fork	Snow Hill	Great Falls	Bluewater	New York	Rocky River	Ft. Bend
Holy Cross	Lakewood	Middle River	Circle	Five Points	Little Falls	Plain City	Three Rivers
Circle	Denver	Forest Hill	Park City		West Point	Pleasant Valley	Bay City

Note: Unalphabetized lists are in general order of spelling difficulty.

Capitalize names of cities and towns.
Students should memorize state postal abbreviations. See p. 50.

Ashland, OH	Weed, CA	Frank, PA	Coldwater, MI	Rush City, MN
Sandy, OR	Bay Park, NY	Hong Kong	New Roads, LA	Salt Lake City, UT
Belt, MT	Clark Fork, MT	Hot Springs, SD	River Grove, IL	Spring Valley, NY
Bend, OR	Clark, SD	House Springs, MO	Riverside, NJ	Sun City, AZ
Kent, OH	Grant Park, IL	Long Pine, NE	Silver Springs, MD	Tell City, IN
Taft, CA	Walker, MN	Red Bank, NJ	Silver, MO	Valley City, ND
West Bend, WI	Ash Fork, AZ	Red Wing, MN	Stillwater, MN	Crown Point, IN
West Branch, MI	Cork, Ireland	Rock Springs, WY	Sweetwater, TN	East Point, GA
Bath, NY	Elm Fork, TX	Sand Springs, OK	Two Rivers, WI	Elk Point, SD
Flint, MI	North Bend, OR	Sandy Springs, GA	White Center, WA	Fox Point, WI
Mist, OR	Portland, OR	Wink, TX	Winter Park, FL	High Point, NC
Bond, CO	Rockport, MA	Beach, ND	Blue Earth, MN	Kitty Hawk, NC
Brush, CO	Rocky Ford, CO	East Bay, TX	Green Meadows, MD	Point Hope, AK
Golf, IL	Rolling Hills, CA	Palm Beach, FL	Pleasant Grove, AL	Sandy Point, TX
Oshkosh, WI	South Bend, IN	West Palm Beach FL	Pleasant View, UT	South Point, MI
Flat Rock, MI	South Gate, CA	Reading, MA	White Earth, ND	West Point, VA
Grants Pass, OR	South Park, KY	Sea Cliff, NY	Highland Park, IL	Mountain Grove, MO
Rockland, ME	St. Cloud, MN	Cape Town, S. Africa	Highland, PA	Mountain View, CA
Ross, OH	Three Forks, MT	Flower Hill, NY	Friend, NE	Jackson, MS
Sunset, UT	York, England	Old Town, ME	Youngstown, NY	Johnson City, NY
Bell, CA	Blue Ash, OH	Cody, WY	Burns, OR	Forest City, IA
Teller, AK	Goodland, KS	Hooper, UT	Sugar City, CO	Grand Prairie, TX
Wells, NV	Roy, NM	New Meadows, ID	Circle, AK	Lake Forest, IL
Baker, MT	Ruth, NV	White Plains, NY	Maple Heights, OH	Park Forest, IL
Cape Cod, MA	Sand Hook, NJ	Brookfield, IL	Bay City, TX	Southern Pines, NC
Lake Bluff, IL	Sandy Hook, CT	New York, NY	Big Bear City, CA	Western Port, MD
St. James, MO	Post, TX	Springfield, IL	Central Valley, NY	Park Ridge, IL
Lakeside, CA	Camp Wood, TX	West View, PA	Cherry City, PA	Central City, KY
Price, UT	Evergreen, AL	Bell Gardens, CA	Cherry Grove, OR	Bridgeport, CT
State Line, MN	Homewood, AL	Broken Bow, OK	Clay City, KY	Candle, AK
Bay Mills, MI	Lakewood, CO	Great Bend, KS	Dade City, FL	Twin Bridges, MT
Bayside, MA	Seven Hills, OH	Great Falls, MT	Elk City, OK	Honey Grove, TX
Cape May, NJ	Wood, SD	Great Neck, NY	Fall City, WA	Key West, FL
Clay, KY	Woodland, CA	Orange City, IA	Hill City, KS	Ruby, AK
Gladstone, NJ	White Cloud, MI	Orange, CA	King City, CA	Independence, MO
Globe, AZ	White Hall, IL	Sunnyside, UT	Lake City, FL	Forest Heights, MD
Homer, AK	Overland Park, KS	Holly Springs, MS	Mound City, IL	Lemon Heights, CA
Hope, AR	Overland, MO	Holly, MI	Ocean City, MD	International Falls, MN
Hopewell, VA	Downs, KS	Hollywood, CA	Ocean Grove, NJ	National City, CA
Nome, AK	Banks, OR	Piper, AL	Ocean Springs, MS	State College, PA
Robe, WA	Big Spring, TX	St. John, IN	Park City, UT	Canyon, CA
Rome, Italy	Black Springs, Australia	Center, TX	Pine City, MN	Council Bluffs, IA
Rose Tree, PA	Camp Springs, MD	Clay Center, KS	Plain City, UT	Council Grove, KS
Speed, IN	Cape Fear, NC		Plant City, FL	
Speedway, IN				

Fort..................Ft.	Ft. Bend, TX	Ft. Kent, ME	Ft. Worth, TX	St. Cloud, MN
Point...............Pt.	Ft. Bliss, TX	Ft. Mill, SC	Pt. Barrow, AK	St. Joseph, MO
Saint ....St.	Ft. Branch, IN	Ft. Smith, AR	Pt. Hope, AK	St. Paul, MN

Note: Unalphabetized lists are in general order of spelling difficulty.

Capitalize names of streets, highways, roads, avenues, etc.

Abbreviations

Avenue ...... Ave.	
Boulevard.Blvd.	
Circle...........Cir.	
Court ....Ct.	
Drive ....Dr.	
Heights ....Hts.	
Highway... Hwy.	
Lane.............Ln.	
Park ....Pk.	
Place............Pl.	
Point ....Pt.	
Road ....Rd.	
Route...........Rt.	
Square .... Sq.	
Street ....St.	
Fourth.......... 4th	
East................E.	
West..............W.	
North ....N.	
South .... S.	

Ashland Drive
Chess Drive
Cliffside Drive
Sunrise Drive
Sunset Drive
West Drive
Ash Place
Candy Place
Drake Drive
Glade Place
James Drive
Kim Place
Midland Place
Fireweed Lane
Hillside Drive
Lakeside Drive
Price Lane
Short Street
Baker Street
Bill Street
Creekside Street
Elm Street
Greenland Dr.

Jade Street
Lee Street
Mike Street
State Street
Card Street
Clark Street
Park Place
Bluebell Drive
Dogwood Street
Driftwood St.
Evergreen St.
Greenwood St.
Redwood Place
Westwood Dr.
Wildwood Lane
Bayshore Drive
Whitehall Street
King Street
Frank Street
Long Street
Windsong Drive
Brown Street
Snowbird Drive

Hood Court
Snowflake Dr.
Main Street
Golden View
Drive
Little Creek Dr.
Center Street
Cross Road
Lucky Road
Post Road
Sand Lake Rd.
Pleasant Drive
Highland Drive
Highway 34
Friendly Lane
Bench Court
Brink Court
Clay Court
Cliff Court
Dane Court
Landmark Court
Sundown Court
Bates Circle

Bay Circle
Bay View Circle
Blackstone Circle
Cape Circle
Circle Drive
Creek Circle
Dale Circle
Drum Circle
Foothill Circle
Fred Circle
Jay Circle
Jeff Circle
Joy Circle
Lake Park Cir.
Lane Circle
Lost Circle
Nash Circle
Park Hills Circle
Parkridge Circle
Starlight Circle
Sugar Circle
Sunny Circle
Wells Circle

Country Club
Lane
Happy Lane
Big Mountain Dr.
Captain Cook Dr.
Benson Blvd.
Forest Drive
Edgewater Cir.
Ridgeview Dr.
View Heights Way
College Drive
Autumn Lane
Cook Avenue
Dare Avenue
Hunt Avenue
Jones Avenue
Northwestern Ave.
Northwind Avenue
Peck Avenue
Rainbow Avenue
Rand Avenue
Ship Avenue

Capitalize names of parks.

Rock Creek Park, DC
Stone Mountain Park, FL
Central Park, NY
College Park, MD
Badlands National Park, SD
Big Bend National Park, TX

Canyonlands National Park, UT
Everglades National Park, FL
Grand Canyon National Park, AZ
Hot Springs National Park, AR
Kings Canyon National Park, CA
Lake Clark National Park, AK

Redwood National Park, CA
Riding Mountain National Park, Can.
Rocky Mountain National Park, CO
Wind Cave National Park, SD
Yellowstone National Park, WY

Capitalize names of oceans and seas.

Arctic Ocean	Pacific Ocean	Black Sea	North Sea	White Sea	East China Sea
Indian Ocean	Atlantic Ocean	Dead Sea	Red Sea	Yellow Sea	South China Sea

Capitalize names of bays and other bodies of water.

James Bay, Canada
Black Bay, Canada
Camps Bay, S. Africa
Fisher Bay, Canada
West Bay, FL
Broken Bay, Australia
Green Bay, WI

North Bay, Canada
Blue Mud Bay, Australia
White Bay, Canada
Hooper Bay, AK
Lower New York Bay, NY
Upper New York Bay, NY
Silver Bay, MN

Long Point Bay, Canada
Hudson Bay, Canada
Two Prairie Bay, AR
Half Moon Bay, CA
Table Bay, S. Africa
Bay of Islands, Canada

Other
Case Inlet, WA
Cook Inlet, AK
Corner Inlet, Australia
Cross Sound
Long Island Sound
English Channel

Note: Unalphabetized lists are in general order of spelling difficulty.

Capitalize names of rivers.

Blue Nile, Africa
Bad River, SD
Bar River, Can.
Bear River, UT
Bell River, Can.
Big Black River, MS
Big Blue River, NE
Big Fork River, MN
Big Hole River, MT
Big Muddy River, IL
Big Sandy River, AZ
Big Sunflower River, MS
Big Wood River, ID
Black River, SC
Blind River, Can.
Blue River, MO
Broad River, GA
Clearwater River, ID
Copper River, AK
Crow Wing River, MN
Dan River, NC
Dane River, England

Deep River, NC
Deep Fork River, OK
Don River, Can.
Dove River, England
Duck River, TN
Eleven Point River, MO
Elk River, WV
Elm River, SD
Fall River, MA
Feather River, CA
Flint River, GA
Fox River, IL
Grand River, MO
Green River, KY
High River, Can.
Hood River, OR
James River, VA
John Day River, OR
Jump River, WI
Ken River, India
Kings River, CA
Leaf River, MS

Lost River, OR
Mad River, CA
Middle River, MD
Milk River
Muddy River, UT
Nan River, Thailand
Nile River, Africa
Orange River, Africa
Park River, ND
Peace River, Can.
Pine River, WI
Raft River, ID
Ram River, Can.
Red River, TN
Red Rock River, MT
Rock River, IA
Rocky River, OH
Root River, WI
Rough River, KY
Rum River, MN
Salt River, AZ
Sand River, S. Africa

Seal River, Can.
Skunk River, IA
Slave River, Can.
Smoky River, Can.
Snake River, ID
South River, NC
Spoon River, IL
Spring River, AR
Sun River, MT
Swan River, MT
Swift River, ME
Test River, England
Thief River, MN
Trent River, England
Walker River, NV
White Nile, Africa
White River, TX
Wild Rice River, MN
Wind River, WY
Wood River, IL
Yellow River, China
Yellowstone River, WY

Capitalize names of creeks, brooks, etc.

Baker Creek, IL
Belt Creek, MT
Berry Creek, Can.
Big Creek, OH
Big Sandy Creek, CO
Buck Creek, IN
Crab Creek. WA
Fall Creek, IN
Fish Creek, LA
Lick Creek, IN
Mill Creek, Can.

Nine Mile Creek, UT
Pine Creek, NV
Rock Creek, WA
Ross Creek, Can.
Salt Creek, IL
Shades Creek, AL
Trim Creek, IL
Horse Creek, CO
South Creek, Australia
Trout Creek, OR
Bound Brook, NJ

Crooked Creek, IL
Pine Brook, NJ
Forked Creek, IN
Clear Creek, TX
Spring Creek, NV
Cow Creek, OR
Bear Brook, Can.
Goose Creek, ID
Crow Creek, CO
Peace Creek, FL
Big Muddy Creek, MT

Clear Boggy Creek, OK
Muddy Creek, UT
Silver Creek, IN
Badwater Creek, WY
Corner Brook, Can.
Sugar Creek, MO
Fountain Creek, CO
Mountain Brook, AL
Twenty Mile Creek, Can.
Cripple Creek, CO
Maple Creek, Can.

Capitalize names of waterfalls.

Rock Falls, IL
Pine Falls, Can.
Red Lake Falls, MN
Fall Creek Falls, TN
Park Falls, WI

Yellowstone Falls, WY
Great Falls, VA
Ribbon Falls, CA
Blackwater Falls, WV

Black River Falls, WI
River Falls, AL
Thief River Falls, MN
American Falls, ID

Valley Falls, KS
Central Falls, RI
Ocean Falls, Can.
Angel Falls, Venezuela

Note: Unalphabetized lists are in general order of spelling difficulty.

Capitalize names of lakes.

Big Lake, WA	Wind Lake, WI	Wild Rice Lake, MN	Summer Lake, OR
Black Lake, NY	Yale Lake, WA	Bear Lake, ID	Tupper Lake, NY
Cross Lake, Can.	Round Lake, IL	Goose Lake, CA	Upper Lake, NV
Duck Lake, Can.	Bighorn Lake, MT	Crow Lake, Can.	Upper Red Lake, MN
Fox Lake, IL	Storm Lake, IA	Dale Hollow Lake, TN	Center Hall Lake, TN
Grand Lake, LA	Torch Lake, MI	Lower Lake, CA	Meadow Lake, Can.
Lake Chad, Africa	Trout Lake, MI	Lower Red Lake, MN	Silver Lake, MA
Pine Flat Lake, CA	Worth Lake, TX	Snow Lake, Can.	Pleasant Lake, NY
Red Lake, MN	Cold Lake, Can.	Rainy Lake	High Rock Lake, NC
Rib Lake, WI	Lake of the Woods	Great Bear Lake, Can.	Burns Lake, Can.
Rice Lake, MN	White Lake, Can.	Great Bitter Lake, Egypt	Last Mountain Lake, Can.
Ross Lake, WA	Swan Lake, Can.	Great Salt Lake, UT	Honey Lake, CA
Sandy Lake, Can.	Gull Lake, Can.	Great Slave Lake, Can.	Island Lake, Can.
Walker Lake, NV	Clear Lake, CA	Orange Lake, FL	Rocky Island Lake, Can.

Capitalize names of mountains and mountain ranges.

Alps, Europe	Clear Hills, Can.	Great Smoky Mountains	Stone Mountain, GA
Sand Hills, NE	Front Range Mountains, CO	Bells Mountain, WA	Table Mountain, S. Africa
Cub Hills, Can.	Mt. Bang, AZ	Big Belt Mountains, MT	Three Sisters Mountains, OR
Pine Hill, NJ	East Hills, NY	Bighorn Mountains	White Mountains, NH
Red Hill, CA	Grays Peak, CO	Blue Mountain, Can.	Wind Mountain, NM
Rock Hill, SC	Kings Peak, UT	Blue Mountains	Wood Mountain, Can.
Rocky Hill, NJ	Longs Peak, CO	Copper Mountain, AK	Forest Hill, PA
Far Hills, NJ	Pikes Peak, CO	Crown Mountain, Can.	Pine Forest Range, NV
Mars Hill, ME	Birds Hill, Can.	Duck Mountain, Can.	Blue Ridge Mountains
Mt. Hope, NJ	Knob Peak, Philippines	Gold Mountain, WA	Pine Ridge, VA
Cloud Peak, WY	Snow Hill, MD	Green Mountain, OR	Independence Mountains, NV
Horn Hill, England	Great Sand Hills, Can.	Kings Mountain, SC	North College Hill, OH
Mt. Rushmore, SD	Lost River Range, ID	Long Range Mountains, Can.	Cherry Hill, NJ
North Hills, NY	Boggy Peak, Antigua	New Hope Mountain, AL	Alaska Range, AK
South Hills, VA	Duckwater Peak, NV	Ray Mountains, AK	Castle Peak, CO
Mt. Cook, New Zealand	Mt. Baker, WA	Rocky Mountains	Iron Mountain, MI
Mt. Hood, OR	Silver Hill, MD	Round Top Mountain, OR	Mt. St. Bride, Can.
Gold Hill, Panama	Mt. Pleasant, TX	Ruby Mountains, NV	Mt. St. Helens, WA
Bush Hill, VA	High Peak, Philippines	Shades Mountain, AL	New England Range,
Swan Hill, Canada	Temple Hills, MD	Silver Star Mountain, WA	
Brooks Range, AK			

Capitalize names of valleys and canyons.

Death Valley, CA	Red River Valley	Big Canyon, TX	Grand Canyon, AZ
Fort Valley, GA	Rock Valley, IA	Big Horn Canyon, MT	Hell's Canyon, ID
Fountain Valley, CA	Spring Valley, MN	Black Canyon, CO	Wind River Canyon, WY
Fox Valley, Australia	Water Valley, MS	Glen Canyon, AZ	Yellowstone Canyon, WY
Mill Valley, CA			

Note: Unalphabetized lists are in general order of spelling difficulty.

Capitalize names of caves or caverns.

Cave of the Mounds, WI   Jewel Cave, SD   Mammoth Cave, KY   Oregon Caves, OR   Wind Cave, SD

Capitalize names of forests.

Big River State Forest, IL	Bighorn National Forest, WY	Holly Springs National Forest, MS
Black Forest, Germany	Black Hills National Forest, WY	Medicine Bow National Forest, WY
Hidden Springs State Forest, IL	Clearwater National Forest, ID	Mt. Baker National Forest, WA
Trail of Tears State Forest, IL	Flathead National Forest, MT	Pike National Forest, CO
Sand Ridge State Forest, IL	Green Mountain National Forest, VT	White River National Forest, CO

Capitalize names of islands.

Baker Island, Oceania	Cat Island, Bahamas	Great Corn Island	North Island, New Zealand
Banks Island, Can.	Channel Islands, CA	Great Duck Island, Can.	Pie Island, Can.
Bell Island, Can.	Christmas Island	Greenland	Rock Island, IL
Berry Islands, Bahamas	City Island, NY	High Island, MI	Ross Island, Can.
Big Island, Can.	Cook Islands	Hog Island, MI	Sand Island, WI
Bird Island, S. Africa	Dog Island, Can.	Horse Islands, Can.	Sea Islands, GA
Bird Rock, Bahamas	Easter Island	Hunter Islands, Australia	Seal Island, S. Africa
Black Island, Can.	Fire Island, NY	King Island, AK	South Fox Island, MI
Blake Island	Fox Island, WA	Long Island, NY	Sugar Island, MI
Block Island, RI	Garden Island, MI	Near Islands, AK	
Blue Island, IL	Grand Island, MI		

Capitalize names of deserts and other geographical features.

Deserts	Rocks	Beaches	Other
Black Rock Desert	Black Rock, UT	Moss Beach, CA	Big Stone Gap, VA
Great Salt Lake Desert, UT	Castle Rock, WA	Ninety Mile Beach, Australia	Copper Cliff, Can.
Great Sandy Desert, OR	Seal Rocks, CA	Seal Beach, CA	Red Pass, Can.
Painted Desert, AZ		Warm Beach, WA	High Prairie, Can.
Smoke Creek Desert, NV			Snake River Plain, ID
			Kings Point, NY
			Cape Cod, MA
			Cape of Good Hope, Afr.
			Cape Horn, Chile

Capitalize names of heavenly bodies.

Planets	Stars
Mercury	Alpha Centauri
Venus	North Star
Earth	
Mars	**Constellations**
Jupiter	Big Dipper
Uranus	Little Dipper
Neptune	Orion
Pluto	Southern Cross

Note: Earth, Sun and Moon are *not* capitalized unless used in a list of other planets or heavenly bodies.

Note: Unalphabetized lists are in general order of spelling difficulty.

Capitalize names of bridges.

13th Street Bridge, KY	Dent Bridge, ID	Main Street Bridge, FL	Red River Bridge, LA
35th Street Bridge, WV	Golden Gate Bridge, CA	Mount Hope Bridge, RI	Ship Canal Bridge, WA
Bear Mountain Bridge, NY	Jamestown Bridge, RI	Newport Bridge, KY	West End Bridge, PA

Capitalize names of schools and colleges.

American River College, CA	Golden Gate College, CA	National Business College, VA
Baker College, OR	Grace College, IN	National College of Education, IL
Bates College, ME	Grand View College, IA	Northern State College, SD
Black Hawk College, IL	College of Great Falls, MT	Pace College, NY
Black Hills State College, SD	Green Mountain College, VT	Prairie State College, IL
Blue Mountain College, MS	Grove City College, PA	College of the Redwoods, CA
Central College, KS	Holy Family College, CA	College of St. Mary, NE
City College of New York, NY	Jones College, FL	Southwestern College, OK
College of the Desert, CA	Lake Forest College, IL	Western College for Women, OH

Brown School, MI	Star of the Sea School, HI	North Pole Middle School, AK
Drake School, ND	Stone School, VA	Country Hills School, FL
East Port School, TN	Third Street School, NJ	Holy Family School, LA
Frost School, IN	Welcome School, SC	Five Points School, PA
King School, WI	West Woods School, AR	Bear Mountain School, CA
Lake Street School, ME	White Plains School, AL	Blue Mountain School, VT
Lakeside School, KY	Field School, MO	Brothers School, OR
Love School, WA	Park View School, CO	Forest Park School, NY
Morningside School, TX	Red Water School, MS	Prairie View School, KS
North High School, CO	Deadwood School, SD	Central Middle School, ID
Pike Lake School, MN	Pleasant Hill School, IA	City Park Middle School, GA
Rand School, WV	Light School, OH	Social Street School, RI
Rock Springs, NC	Young School, IL	Grand Island School, NE
Second Hill Lane School, CT	Bird Middle School, MA	Independent School, MT
Spring Creek School, NV	Gray Middle School, OK	Southern Heights School, NM
St. James School, MD	Main Street Middle School, NH	Desert View School, WY

Note: All schools are elementary schools unless otherwise indicated.

Capitalize names of stores.

Safeway	Pay n Save	Payless Drug	Midnight Sun	Mapco
Foodland	K Mart	Store	Boat Shop	Costco

Capitalize names of museums.

Portland Art Museum, ME	National Air and Space Museum, DC	American Museum of Science, TN
Children's Museum, MA	Air Force Museum, OH	Museum of Modern Art, NY City
Museum of Science, MA	Football Hall of Fame, OH	National Museum of American
Baseball Hall of Fame Museum, NY	Great Plains Zoo and Museum, SD	History, DC

Note: Unalphabetized lists are in general order of spelling difficulty.

Capitalize names of hospitals, churches, hotels, motels.

Hospitals
North Star Hospital
Holy Family Hospital
Central State Hospital
Kent General Hospital

Churches
Parkside Church
Church of God
First Church of God
Church of the Living God

Hotels & Motels
Bay View Inn
Super 8
Hotel Captain Cook
Best Western
Hillside Motel

Golden North Motel
Red Ram Motel
South Seas Hotel
Woods Motel
Motel 6

Capitalize names of libraries.

Blue Island Public Library
East Point Public Library
Forest Park Public Library
Long Ridge Public Library
Mountain Home Public Library
Page Public Library

Prairie Creek Public Library
Pretty Prairie Public Library
Snowflake Town Library
State Law Library
Sugar Grove Public Library
Sun City Library

Twin Falls Public Library
White City Public Library
Winter Park Public Library
Young Public Library
Leisure World Library
National Library of Medicine

Capitalize names of restaurants.

Top of the World
Chuck E. Cheese
Red Apple
Lunch Box

Cozy Corner
Lucky Wishbone
The Perfect Cup
Rice Bowl

Godfathers
Village Inn
Arctic Rose Restaurant
Beef and Sea Restaurant

Flight Deck Restaurant
Golden Pond Restaurant
White Spot Restaurant

Capitalize names of other man-made structures.

Big Bend Dam, SC
Fort Peck Dam, MT
White House, DC

Great Wall of China
World Trade Center, NY
Grand Canal, China

Hood Canal, WA
Hoover Dam, NV
John Day Dam, OR

Rock Island Dam, WA
Sears Tower, IL
Superdome, LA

Capitalize names of days *(Spelling Plus list 43).*

Sunday
Monday

Tuesday
Wednesday

Thursday
Friday

Saturday

Capitalize names of months *(Spelling Plus list 52).*

January
February
March

April
May
June

July
August
September

October
November
December

Capitalize names of holidays.

New Year's Day
Ground Hog Day
Good Friday

Easter
Mother's Day
Flag Day

Father's Day
Independence Day
Fourth of July

Thanksgiving
Halloween
Christmas

Note: Unalphabetized lists are in general order of spelling difficulty.

POSTAL ABBREVIATIONS

Alabama	AL	Montana	MT
Alaska	AK	Nebraska	NE
Arizona	AZ	Nevada	NV
Arkansas	AR	New Hampshire	NH
California	CA	New Jersey	NJ
Colorado	CO	New Mexico	NM
Connecticut	CT	New York	NY
Delaware	DE	North Carolina	NC
Florida	FL	North Dakota	ND
Georgia	GA	Ohio	OH
Hawaii	HI	Oklahoma	OK
Idaho	ID	Oregon	OR
Illinois	IL	Pennsylvania	PA
Indiana	IN	Rhode Island	RI
Iowa	IA	South Carolina	SC
Kansas	KS	South Dakota	SD
Kentucky	KY	Tennessee	TN
Louisiana	LA	Texas	TX
Maine	ME	Utah	UT
Maryland	MD	Vermont	VT
Massachusetts	MA	Virginia	VA
Michigan	MI	Washington	WA
Minnesota	MN	West Virginia	WV
Mississippi	MS	Wisconsin	WI
Missouri	MO	Wyoming	WY

MONTHS

January	Jan.
February	Feb.
March	Mar.
April	Apr.
May	May
June	June
July	July
August	Aug.
September	Sept.
October	Oct.
November	Nov
December	Dec.

DAYS

Sunday	Sun.
Monday	Mon.
Tuesday	Tues.
Wednesday	Wed.
Thursday	Thurs.
Friday	Fri.
Saturday	Sat.

COMMON ABBREVIATIONS

Avenue	Ave.	Heights	Hts.	Point	Pt.
Boulevard	Blvd.	Highway	Hwy.	Post Office	P.O.
care of (in care of)	c/o	Incorporated	Inc.	postscript	P.S.
Circle	Cir.	Junior	Jr.	President	Pres.
Company	Co.	Lane	Ln.	Reverend	Rev.
Corporation	Corp.	Limited	Ltd.	Road	Rd.
Court	Ct.	medical doctor	M.D.	Room	Rm.
Department	Dept.	Missus	Mrs.	Route	Rt.
Doctor	Dr.	Mister	Mr.	Saint	St.
Drive	Dr.	Miz	Ms.	Senior	Sr.
Fort	Ft.	Mount	Mt.	Square	Sq.
General	Gen.	Park	Pk.	Street	St.
Governor	Gov.	Place	Pl.	University	Univ.

PUNCTUATION

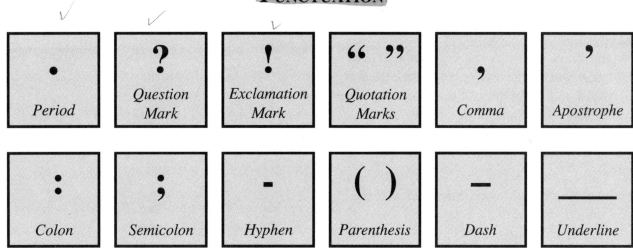

| Period | Question Mark | Exclamation Mark | Quotation Marks | Comma | Apostrophe |

| Colon | Semicolon | Hyphen | Parenthesis | Dash | Underline |

The marks shown above are to assist readers in recognizing punctuation marks. The rules below are for the punctuation marks most often used. Most dictionaries contain complete rules of punctuation.

PUNCTUATION TO END SENTENCES

1. To end a **statement**, a sentence that tells, use a period (**.**).
2. To end a **question**, a sentence that asks, use a question mark (**?**).
3. To end an **exclamation**, a sentence that expresses strong feeling, use an exclamation point (**!**).
4. To end a **command**, a sentence that tells someone to do something, use a period (**.**).

USES OF PERIODS

Use periods:
1. To end statements or commands. *Please come here.*
2. In bibliography cards or entries. See page 38 for examples.
3. After initials. *A. R. Smith*
4. After most abbreviations. *A.D., B.C., Mr.* See page 52 for a list of common abbreviations.
5. After numbers or letters of a list.

USES OF APOSTROPHES

Use apostrophes:
1. In contractions, to show letters have been left out. *didn't, o'clock*
2. To show possession. *Mary's book* Use *s'* with plural nouns. *the boys' coats*
3. To pluralize letters or numbers. *A's, 5's*

USES OF COLONS

Use colons:
1. After the salutation in a business letter. See page 37 for an example.
2. Between place of publication and publisher in a bibliography entry. See page 38.
3. To introduce a long list of items.

USES OF HYPHENS

Use hyphens:
1. In writing numbers from *twenty-one* to *ninety-nine*.
2. To divide words at the end of a line. The rules for correctly dividing words are complicated. Avoid it when possible.

PUNCTUATION OF DIRECT QUOTATIONS

1. Use quotation marks (" ") to enclose the **exact words** a person says in a direct quotation. Remember to capitalize the first word of a direct quotation.
"This book is interesting," said Jane.
Jane said, "This book is interesting."
"This book," said Jane, "is interesting."

2. Use a comma (**,**) to set off direct quotations from expressions such as *he said* and *she replied*. Words that can be used instead of *said* include: *announced, answered, asked, commanded, demanded, drawled, echoed, exclaimed, giggled, growled, grumbled, hissed, howled, insisted, laughed, chuckled, moaned, mumbled, murmured, muttered, ordered, pleaded, protested, remarked, repeated, replied, roared, screamed, shouted, sighed, snapped, snarled, squeaked, squealed, stammered, stated, whimpered, whined, whispered, yelled.*

3. Use a period (**.**) placed inside the quotation marks when the end of a quoted sentence is the end of the written sentence.
Martha said, "I think this is the right way."

4. Replace the period at the end of a direct quotation with a comma (**,**) when the end of a quoted statement is **not** the end of the sentence. The comma is placed inside the quotation marks.
"I think this is the right way," said Martha.

5. When the quoted sentence is a question or exclamation, use a question mark (**?**) or exclamation point (**!**) placed inside the quotation marks even if the end of the quotation is not the end of the sentence.
"Look out!" shouted Jane.
Steven asked, "Where are my skates?"

USES OF COMMAS

Use commas:
1. In direct quotations. See "Punctuating Direct Quotations," to the left.
2. In letters. See pages 36–37.
3. In bibliography cards or entries. See p. 38.
4. Between the day of the week and the date.
Monday, March 4
5. Between the date and the year.
July 4, 1776
6. Between city and state. *Tampa, Florida*
7. Between city and country.
London, England
8. After a person's last name when written before the first name (as in a telephone book or encyclopedia). *Lincoln, Abraham Smith, Larry*
9. Between items in a series of three or more. *She can sing, dance, and play the saxophone.*
10. After words that introduce a sentence, such as *yes, no, oh, well, first,* and so on. *Well, I guess so.*
11. Before certain words that end a sentence, such as *etc., too,* and *also.*
May I come, too?
12. To separate the name of the person to whom you are talking from the rest of the sentence. *Mom, are you ready to go?*
I understand what you mean, Mr. Jones.
This, Mike, is for you.
13. Before such words as *and, but* and *or* in a compound sentence (a sentence made by combining two shorter sentences). *The roads are icy today, and there have been several accidents.*
14. To separate "parenthetical" words or phrases, such as *of course, however.* See p. 14 for more examples. These words and phrases add meaning, but the sentence would be a complete sentence without them. *This book, however, is very useful. You are right, of course!*

PREFIXES AND SUFFIXES

One of the marks of a successful speller is an understanding of word construction. At a basic level, this helps with the spelling of homophones such as *tacks – tax* and *toad – towed*. Students should learn to recognize base words and identify words to which a prefix or suffix has been added.

Inflectional endings in English are used to pluralize nouns, and to show tense of verbs:

1. Add *-s* or *-es* to pluralize most nouns. Use *-es* rather than *-s* when the base noun ends with the sound of *s, x, z, sh,* or *ch.*
2. Add *-s* to present tense verbs after the third person singular *(he, she, it)*. For example, *You play but he/she/it plays.*
3. Add *-ed* to form regular past tense verbs: *They played.*
4. Add *-ing* to form the present participle: *We are playing.*

This section lists common suffixes and prefixes, along with words from the *Spelling Plus* list to which they can be added to form another word. If the affix is introduced in *Spelling Plus,* the list is indicated. Use words students have previously learned to spell. A small superscript number next to a word shows that it is the first word from that level list. For example: point[5] means that the word *point* is the first word on a Level 5 list to which that suffix can be added. Although words are assigned to levels primarily for use in a schoolwide program, these designations can help you gauge when to introduce an affix.

Post a list of these suffixes and prefixes with their meanings on the wall of the classroom and check them off as they're introduced!

Here is a **general lesson plan** for teaching suffixes and prefixes:

1. Write a word with the affix on the board. Have students identify the base word and determine whether the affix is a suffix or prefix. Remember that *pre-* means "before."
2. Define the prefix or suffix. How does it change the meaning of the word? Can you think of some other words with this prefix/suffix? Discuss.
3. Have students write and add the affix to words you dictate which don't require a change in the base word.
4. If necessary, review the appropriate rules for adding suffixes.
5. Dictate and have students write words in which the base word must be changed before adding the suffix.
6. Prefixes generally do not affect the spelling of the base word. However, the spelling of a prefix may change depending on the base word. For example: *in-* (not) changes to *il-* before *l* as in *illegal,* to *im-* before *p, b,* and *m* as in *impossible,* and to *ir-* before *r* as in *irrelevant.* See p. 62.
7. After a prefix or suffix has been introduced, have students search for examples of its use in books or newspapers.
8. Use words with the affixes you've introduced in dictation. Ask students to identify the base word and the affix, then recall the meaning of the affix each time it's dictated for awhile.

Upper-grade teachers may challenge students to memorize the meanings of the most common prefixes and suffixes, as well as Greek and Latin word roots, a few at a time. Lists of these are on pp. 56–57 and 78.

PREFIXES

A **prefix** is a word part that can be added to the beginning of a base word to change its meaning or to form a new word.

Prefix	Meaning	Examples
ab-	away, off	abnormal, absent
ad-	toward, to	admit, advance
aero-	air	aerobatics, aerospace
ante-	before	antedate, anteroom
anti-	against	antiseptic, antiaircraft
anthropo-	human	anthropology
astro-	star	astronomy, astronaut
auto-	self, own	autograph, automatic
bi-	two	bicycle, biweekly
bio-	life	biography, biology
centi-	hundred	centigram, centipede
circum-	around	circumference
co-	together	cooperate, coordinate
com-	together	combine, compete
con-	together	connect, conversation
contra-	against	contradiction
cosmo-	universe	cosmonaut, cosmic
counter-	against	counteract
de-	from, down	defrost, depress
deca-	ten	decade, decagon
deci-	ten	decimal, decibel
dis-	not	disagree, dishonest
	opposite of	disappear, disconnect
en-	put into	entangle, enjoy
	cause to be	enlarge, enable
equi-	equal	equator, equilateral
ex-	out, from	explode, extend
ex-	former	ex-teacher
extra-	outside of	extraordinary
fore-	before	forewarn, forefathers
geo-	earth	geology, geography
hydro-	water	hydroelectric
hyper-	too much	hyperactive
il-	not	illegal, illogical
im-	not	impossible, impolite
in-	not	incorrect, invisible
	in, into	inject, include
infra-	below	infrared, infrasonic

Prefix	Meaning	Examples
inter-	between	interrupt, intercept
ir-	not	irregular
mal-	bad	malfunction
mega-	great	megaphone, megaton
micro-	small	microscope, microbe
mid-	middle	midnight, midsection
milli-	thousand	millimeter, millipede
mini-	small	miniskirt
mis-	wrong, bad	misspell, mistrust
mono-	one	monotone, monopoly
multi-	many	multicolored
non-	not	nonstop, nonsense
ob-	toward	object, obtain
omni-	all	omnivore, omniscient
out-	more than	outnumber, outdo
over-	too much	oversleep, overflow
poly-	many	polygon, polychrome
post-	after	postscript, postdate
pre-	before	prefix, preschool
pro-	for	pronoun, prolabor
quadr-	four	quadruplet, quadrant
re-	back	refill, repay
	again	rebuild, reconsider
retro-	behind	retroactive, retrospect
semi-	half	semicircular, semisoft
sub-	below	submarine, subzero
super-	above	superpower, superior
sym-, syn-	together	sympathy, synonym
tele-	far off	telephone, television
trans-	across	transport, transect
tri-	three	tricycle, triangle
ultra-	beyond	ultrasonic, ultraviolet
un-	not	unlucky, unsafe
	opposite of	unplug, uncover
under-	below	underground
	not enough	undercooked
uni-	one	universe, uniform
up-	up	uplift, uphill

SUFFIXES

A **suffix** is a word part that is added after a base word to change its meaning or form a new word.

Suffix	Meaning	Examples	Part of Speech
-able, -ible	capable or worthy of being	washable, reversible	adjective
-al	pertaining to	frontal, educational	adjective
-an	one born or living in	American, African	noun, adjective
-ance, -ancy	a thing that is	inheritance	noun
-ant	a person or thing that	accountant	noun
	causing, showing or being	radiant, observant	adjective
-ary	pertaining to, connected with	dictionary, imaginary	noun, adjective
-ate	to become or cause to become	activate, evaporate	verb
	filled with	proportionate	adjective
-dom	state of being	wisdom	noun
-ed	past tense	liked, wanted	verb
-eer	person having to do with	engineer, mountaineer	noun
-en	become, cause to be or have	darken, brighten	verb
	made of	wooden, woolen	adjective
-er	more	taller, wider	adjective
	a person or thing which	miner, roller	noun
-ery	the act of	robbery	noun
-ese	native of, language of	Chinese, Japanese	adjective
-ess	female	lioness, actress	noun
-est	most	biggest, highest	adjective
-ful	full of, having	colorful, careful	adjective
-fy	make or cause to become	simplify, glorify	verb
-hood	condition of	childhood, likelihood	noun
-ian	someone who	musician, politician	noun
-ing	continuous action	listening, running	verb
-ion, -tion	result of, state of being	correction, action	noun
-ish	like, somewhat	childish, foolish	adjective
-ist	person who	novelist, artist	noun
-ity, -ty	state of being	possibility, difficulty	noun
-ize	cause to be	modernize, finalize	verb
-less	without	helpless, restless	adjective
-logy	science of	geology, biology	noun
-ly	like, in a manner that is	friendly, loudly	adverb
-ment	result of being	punishment, pavement	noun
-ness	quality or state of being	happiness, sickness	noun
-ous	full of, having	humorous, dangerous	adjective
-or	person who	actor, sailor	noun
-s, -es	more than one	boys, boxes	noun
-y	like, full of	dusty, wavy	adjective

Suffix *-able, -ible*

This suffix forms an adjective and means "capable or worthy of being." It is introduced on *Spelling Plus* list 63.

After adding *-able* or *-ible*, add *un-*, *-ity*, *-ly*.

GUIDELINE: *One of the most difficult problems in English spelling is **-able** vs. **-ible**. Memorization is necessary. The following may be somewhat helpful:*
-able is more common than -ible.
*-ible is generally not added to a whole word (**break** / **breakable**).*
*-ible is used to keep a **c** or **g** soft (**eligible**, **invincible**).*
*-ible is used if a related word ends in **-ion** (**collection** / **collectible**).*

win[1]	work	touch	excuse
stop	think[3]	laugh	excite
pass	reach	return	explain
live	teach	address	receive
move	season	person[5]	deceive
sale	reason	perfect	escape
like	clean	notice	imagine
size	read	entertain	describe
pay	allow	enjoy	repeat
play	bear	fasten	identify
note	wear	climb	approach
close	know	answer	achieve
love	show	bridge	control
use	believe	force	recognize
warm[2]	break	argue	
start	catch[4]	build	terrible
find	watch	sense	responsible
forget	measure	question	possible
understand	learn	accept[6]	impossible

Normally, drop silent **e**: likable, movable.
To keep **c** and **g** soft, retain the **e**: noticeable, peaceable, replaceable, changeable, manageable, knowledgeable.

Suffix *-al*

This suffix forms an adjective and means "pertaining to."
After adding *-al*, try adding *-ize*, *-ly*.

front[2]	incident	nation
person[5]	accident	occasion
direction	procedure	profession
addition	continue	
music[6]	education	

Suffix *-en*

This suffix forms a verb and means "become, cause to be or have."
After adding *-en*, try adding *-ed* or *-ing*.

red[1]	deep[2]	strength	light
black	dark	weak	tight
sick	hard	loose	tough
quick	short	smooth	
wide	length[3]	dead[4]	

Suffix *-er*

This suffix forms a noun and means "a person or thing which."
After adding *-er*, try adding *-s*.

plan[1]	grade	open	catch[4]	listen
help	time	think[3]	watch	doubt
win	play	speak	stretch	climb
quit	love	teach	board	build
stop	come	cheat	search	island
drop	use	lead	learn	develop[6]
cut	feel[2]	clean	fight	spell
run	start	read	buy	receive
check	talk	begin	write	foreign
call	walk	room	wreck	repeat
tell	ground	blow	point[5]	achieve
give	find	wait	destroy	perform
move	lose	view	forest	
fly	work	believe	fasten	

[1]These words are listed in the order that they are introduced in *Spelling Plus*. The numbers which follow some words indicate that they are the first word on that level list.

Suffixes -er and -est

These suffixes are added to adjectives and mean "more" *(-er)*, and "most" *(-est)*. They are introduced on *Spelling Plus* list 53.

After adding *-er* or *-est*, try adding *un-*.

red[1]	hard	clear	new	hungry
bit	warm	weak	few	lucky
hot	large	clean	great	sorry
black	short	mean	quiet	happy
sick	blue	brown	little[4]	pretty
quick	true	dirty	heavy	noisy[5]
small	old	loose	early	poor
full	cold	soon	light	simple
nice	kind	smooth	tight	guilty
wide	white	slow	high	straight
green[2]	long[3]	yellow	tough	weird[6]
deep	strong	plain	young	
dark	near	fair	busy	

Do *not* use *-er* and *-est* on words with three or more syllables or words which already have a suffix. Use *more* or *most* before these words:

important	careful	innocent	nervous
surprised	complete	difficult	jealous
certain	definite	responsible	serious
often	usual	similar	humorous
central	practical	particular	mischievous
special	immediate	necessary	delicious
interesting	patient	brilliant	convenient
regular	intelligent	peculiar	independent
exciting	convenient	familiar	

Suffix -ful

This suffix forms an adjective and mean "full of, having." Introduced on *Spelling Plus* list 38.

After adding *-ful*, try adding *-ly, -er, -est, un-*.

hand[1]	hope	power	beauty
help	use	watch[4]	duty[5]
wish	arm[2]	wonder	doubt
will	forget	wrong	force
play	care[3]	hurt	success[6]

Suffix -hood

This suffix forms a noun and means "condition."

man	child	sister	brother	woman
state	girl	mother	father	neighbor
boy				

Suffix -ish

This suffix forms a verb and means "like, somewhat."

After adding *-ish*, try adding *-ly*.

red[1]	green[2]	blue	child	yellow
black	dark	boy	brown[3]	young
gray	warm	old	girl	

Suffix -ity or -ty

This suffix forms a noun and means "state of being." Introduced on *Spelling Plus* list 55.

up[1]	safe	difficult	able
real[3]	author	similar	(ability)
certain[5]	actual[6]	peculiar	responsible
special	practical	familiar	identify
final	general	principal	(identity)

Suffix -ty

This suffix is used with numbers and means "times ten." Introduced on *Spelling Plus* list

nine	six	seven	eight

Note: twenty, thirty, forty, fifty

Suffix -ize

This suffix forms a noun and means "cause to be." Introduced on *Spelling Plus* list 67.

After adding *-ize*, try adding *-ation*.

real[3]	hospital	special	general
winter[4]	modern	author	national
weather	character	motor	summary[6]
American	final	regular	apology
private	social[5]	actual	familiar

Suffix *-less*

Forms an adjective and means "without."
After adding *-less,* try adding *-ly.*

help[1]	sleep[2]	heart	noise[5]
name	need	bottom	point
age	mind	water[4]	voice
face	child	head	mother
time	thank[3]	light	father
home	care	friend	doubt
hope	power	purpose	blood
use	window	sugar	speech

Suffix *-ly*

This suffix forms an adverb and means "like or in a manner that is." Sometimes *-al* is needed before *-ly* can be added: profession**al**ly, occasion**al**ly, incident**al**ly, accident**al**ly. After adding *-ly,* try adding *un-, -er.*

man[1]	over	high	actual
hot	strong[3]	private	usual
cost	year	friend	practical
sick	near	wrong	general
quick	dear	purpose	immediate
full	clear	sure	different
name	weak	busy	patient
state	easy	hungry	intelligent
time	real	lucky	independent
nice	clean	happy	convenient
like	loose	perfect[5]	leisure
wide	slow	certain	innocent
home	plain	sister	separate
close	main	mother	similar
love	fair	brother	particular
free[2]	chief	father	national
deep	new	relative	necessary
week	sudden	secret	brilliant
dark	great	poor	nervous
hard	quiet	central	jealous
warm	careful[4]	final	serious
part	awful	social	humorous
large	heavy	guilty	continuous
short	dead	straight	delicious
hour	pleasant	absent	
even	light	regular	simply
most	night	complete[6]	possibly
month	right	extreme	responsibly
open	tight	definite	terribly

Suffix *-ment*

This suffix forms a noun and means "result of being." Introduced on *Spelling Plus* list 59.

move[1]	measure[4]	argument*	disappoint
state	further	excite[6]	embarrass
place	entertain[5]	develop	achieve
pay	enjoy	govern	commit
better[3]			

argument and *judgment* drop the *e*

Suffix *-ness*

This suffix forms a noun and means "quality or state of being."

red[1]	deep	clean	tough
hot	dark	mean	sure
black	hard	smooth	single
sick	warm	slow	happy
quick	short	fair	pretty
small	good	sudden	lonely
still	blue	great	busy
full	cold	quiet	straight[5]
same	kind	heavy[4]	complete[6]
like	white	dead	weird
wide	open	pleasant	separate
gray	near[3]	light	conscious
green[2]	weak	tight	nervous

Suffix *-ion, -tion, -ation*

This suffix forms a noun and means "the act or state of." Introduced on *Spelling Plus* list 64.
After adding *-tion,* try adding *-al* and *-ly.*

grade[1]	continue	profess
note	imagine	possess
act[2]	concentrate	progress
argument[5]	educate	discuss
sense	identify	fascinate
direct	recommend	appreciate
except[6]	exaggerate	
expect	accommodate	describe
suggest	realize	repeat
prepare	success	explain
		pronounce

Suffix -y

This suffix forms an adjective and means "like, full of." Introduced on *Spelling Plus* list 45. After adding -y, try adding -er, -est, -ly, un-.

hand[1]	spring	hair	touch
luck	mean	heart	luck
class	scare	catch[4]	noise[5]
shine	dirt	stretch	point
sleep[2]	room	water	blood
hard	rain	winter	guilt
length[3]	air	might	weight[6]

Prefix de-

This prefix means "from, down."

grade[1]	face	part[2]	board[3]	forest[5]

Prefix dis-

This prefix means "not, opposite of."

like[1]	allow[3]	interest	continue
close	believe	figure	appear
use	cover[4]	similar[6]	possess
arm[2]	able[5]		

Prefix en-, em-

This prefix means "put into or cause to be."

list[1]	act	power	circle	able
large[2]	body[3]	sure[4]	joy[5]	force

Prefix in-, il-, im-, ir-

This prefix means "not." Use different spellings of the prefix depending on the first letter of the root word.

perfect[5]	complete	different	responsible
regular	definite	patient	decision
experience[6]	practical	convenient	

Prefix inter-

This prefix means "between."

state[1]	act[2]	view	library	national[6]
play	school[3]	office[5]	island	college

Prefix mis-

This prefix means "wrong, bad."

led[1]	place	lead[3]	statement[5]
try	fire	read	guess
name	lay	copy	figure
state	use	laid	spell[6]
take	understand[2]		

Prefix out-

This prefix means "more than" in these words:

stand(ing)[1]	live	play	grow
last	do	done	argue[4]
did	shine	wear[3]	guess
run			

It means "out" in these words:

let[1]	side	house[2]	field
cry	lay	look	break
line	come	put	
		reach[3]	

Prefix over-

This prefix means "too much" in these words:

cost[1]	stay	work	build[5]
fill	done	draw	exercise[6]
do	use	throw[3]	develop(ed)
state	sleep[2]	paid	weight
time	stayed	stepped	prepare
size	filled	learn[4]	achieve
pay	doing		

It means "over" in the following words:

hand[1]	come	hear[3]	coming
all	see[2]	sea(s)	heard[4]
take	look	power	night
lay	looked	taking	turn

Prefix pre-

This prefix means "before."

plan[1]	pay	view	write
cut	school[3]	board[4]	writing
game	paid		

Prefix *re-*

This prefix means "back or again." Introduced on *Spelling Plus* list 43.

did[1]	use	view	wrote
run	start[2]	moving	turn
check	called	living	program
call	played	cover[4]	build[5]
tell	filled	type	built
fill	mind	board	sign
live	act	measure	figure
move	draw	search	explain[6]
do	work	learn	direct
take	open	touch	develop
place	think[3]	group	appear
size	teach	write	acquaint
pay	paid	writing	possess
done	new		

Prefix *un-*

This prefix means "not, opposite of."

end(ing)[1]	afraid	fasten
cut	fair	able
do	planned	guard(ed)
name(d)	cover[4]	sign(ed)
made	pleasant	tie
like	earth	tying
said	hurt	interesting
done	sure	exciting[6]
seen[2]	trouble(d)	expect(ed)
true	important	develop(ed)
asked	lucky	usual
kind	happy	intelligent
clear[3]	tried	identify(ed)
easy	hurried	necessary
real	luckily	embarrass(ed)
clean	happiness	equipped
known	notice(d)[5]	familiar
paid	certain	conscious

Prefix *under-*

This prefix means "below, not enough."

hand[1]	take	paid	figure
stand	line	planned	explain[6]
went	pay	cover[4]	develop(ed)
did	arm[2]	water	weight
cut	ground	study	educate(d)
class	stood	secretary[5]	achieve
go	work	statement	commit
state	world	guess	equipped
age	power(ed)[3]	built	

The following prefixes change their spellings depending on the base word. See a dictionary for further information.

in-	*incorrect*
im-	*impossible, immortal, imbalance*
il-	*illegal*
ir-	*irregular*

ad-	*ex-*	*ob-*
ac-	*e-*	*oc-*
af-	*ef-*	*of-*
ag-	*em-*	*op-*
ap-	*es-*	*o-*
ar-		
as-	*syn-*	
at-	*syl-*	
al-	*sym-*	
an-	*sys-*	
con-	*sub-*	
com-	*suc-*	
col-	*suf-*	
cor-	*sug-*	
	sup-	
dis-	*sum-*	
dif-	*sur-*	
dir-		
di-		

GRAMMAR AND PARTS OF SPEECH

Traditional English grammar is based on Latin. At the time the rules of English grammar were formulated, Latin was revered and considered the perfect language. Unfortunately, Latin grammar didn't fit English very well. In English, word order is extremely important. Countless words can be used as either nouns or verbs. In Latin, inflections are much more important. According to *Webster's New World Dictionary,* "The whole theory of parts of speech does not fit English very well, and the traditional definitions of these parts are not sharply applicable to modern American grammar. The concept and the terms stem from Latin, where they were much more appropriate."

Educators must decide how much or how little grammar should be introduced, based on curricular objectives and local expectations. A school staff should consider discussing which aspects of grammar should be taught at which levels. I recommend the following emphases:

Level Three – Homophones
Level Four – Nouns, pronouns, adjectives
Level Five – Review plus verbs and adverbs.
Level Six – Review plus prepositions,
    conjunctions, and interjections.

Some reasons for teaching grammar are:

1. Cultural literacy. An educated American is expected to know the difference between a noun and a verb.
2. Improved understanding of how English works. This may transfer into improvements in writing, but the connection is not direct.
3. Improved understanding of other languages. Many people don't really understand grammar until they study another language. Traditional grammar is more useful in languages that are highly inflected.

Although grammar is a traditional part of the school curriculum, and students should have a basic understanding of it, many people live long productive lives without a thorough knowledge of how the language works. Learning grammar can be compared to learning what makes a computer tick. It is fascinating for some people and of value to almost any user, but not strictly necessary. A person can operate a computer quite competently without in-depth knowledge of how it works. Experts or reference resources can be consulted when problems arise that require this specialized knowledge. Because of time limitations in the classroom, it is important to decide how much grammar needs to be taught and to what level of mastery.

This section is to assist teachers in using the vehicle of dictation to introduce the basics of traditional grammar. The 1000 core words are listed in alphabetical order, with the number of the list on which they're introduced in *Spelling Plus* to the immediate right. If a word is commonly used by children as only *one* part of speech, an asterisk (*) appears in the appropriate column. If it is commonly used as more than one part of speech, the numbers in the columns indicate the order of presentation in the dictionary (roughly the order of frequency of use). When first introducing a part of speech, avoid words that are commonly used as more than one part of speech to prevent confusion.

In addition, words that are used almost exclusively as a single part of speech are listed on pp. 68–69 in order of introduction in *Spelling Plus.* The superscript numeral by some words indicates that it is the first word on a list at that level. For example, road[4] means that *road* is the first noun on a Level 4 list. Use words that students have already learned to spell when introducing parts of speech.

GRAMMAR AND PARTS OF SPEECH

Note: It would be impossible to include a thorough explanation of our complex English language in a short space. This section is intended to provide a simplified framework from which learning can progress, and is not intended to be comprehensive.

Nouns

Definition: A **noun** names a person, place, thing, quality, act or feeling: *girl, city, desk, honesty, sadness*
Nouns may be made up of more than one word: *Dr. Smith, Pikes Peak*

Proper nouns and common nouns:
A **proper noun** names someone or something in particular and is capitalized: *Mary* (See pages 39–51.)
A **common noun** is any noun that is not a proper noun: *girl, city, river*

Singular nouns and plural nouns:
A **singular noun** names <u>one</u> person, place, thing, quality, act or feeling: *hat*
A **plural noun** names more than one: *hats*
Rules for pluralizing words:
1. To form the plural of most nouns, add -*s*: *dogs*
2. For nouns ending in -*s*, -*x*, -*z*, -*sh*, or -*ch*, add -*es*: *buses, foxes, bushes, scratches*
3. For nouns ending in -*o*, add -*s* or -*es*: *radios, potatoes*
4. For nouns ending with a vowel and -*y*, add -*s*: *toys, monkeys*
   For nouns ending with a consonant and -*y*, change the *y* to *i* and add -*es*: *berries, babies*
5. Some nouns form irregular plurals, including the following:

moose – moose	*child – children*	*mouse – mice*
deer – deer	*man – men*	*goose – geese*
fish – fish	*woman – women*	*foot – feet*
sheep – sheep	*person – people*	*tooth – teeth*

Pronouns

Definition: A **pronoun** is a word that takes the place of a noun.

Personal pronouns
A **personal pronoun** refers to a specific person or thing.
Singular pronouns refer to one person, plural pronouns to more than one.
First person pronouns refer to the person speaking or writing.
Second person pronouns refer to the person being spoken or written to.
Third person pronouns refer to any other person or object.
Subject pronouns replace a noun in the subject of the sentence (person or thing doing the action).
Possessive pronouns replace a possessive noun.
Object pronouns replace a noun which is receiving the action of a sentence.

Indefinite pronouns do not refer to a specific person or thing.

anybody	*anyone*	*anything*	*whatever*
everybody	*everyone*	*everything*	*whoever*
somebody	*someone*	*something*	*one*
nobody	*no one*	*nothing*	*you*

Reflexive pronouns refer back to the subject.

myself	*ourselves*
yourself	*yourselves*
himself	*themselves*
herself	
itself	

Possessive nouns
Possessive nouns show ownership: <u>*Mike's*</u> *book*
Rules for forming possessives:
1. To form the possessive of most singular nouns, add '*s*: *Mary* becomes *Mary's*: *Mary's new car is red.*
2. To form the possessive of a plural noun that ends in -*s*, add ': *boys* becomes *boys*': *The boys' mothers were all at school.*
3. To form the possessive of a plural noun which does not end in -*s*, add '*s*: *children* becomes *children's*: *The children's hats were gone.*

Chart of Personal Pronouns

		Singular			Plural	
	Subject	Object	Possessive	Subject	Object	Possessive
First Person	*I*	*me*	*my* *mine*	*we*	*us*	*our* *ours*
Second Person	*you*	*you*	*your* *yours*	*you*	*you*	*your* *yours*
Third Person	*he* *she* *it*	*him* *her* *it*	*his* *her(s)* *its*	*they*	*them*	*their* *theirs*

Adjectives

Definition: An **adjective** describes, or modifies (limits the meaning of), a noun or pronoun: *Three angry people were arguing. She was happy to come home.*

Articles. The **articles** are *a*, *an*, and *the*.

Use *a* before singular nouns beginning with a consonant: *a dog*

Use *an* before singular nouns beginning with a vowel sound: *an egg, an hour*

Use *the* before any noun, to refer to a specific noun: *the milk, the moon*

Comparative and superlative adjectives.

Rules for forming comparative and superlative adjectives:

1. For most adjectives of one or two syllables, add *-er* or *-est* to form comparative and superlative adjectives.
   John is tall.
   Janet is taller than John.
   Mike is the tallest of the three.

2. For longer adjectives, use *more* or *most* to form comparative and superlative adjectives.
   Monica is discouraged.
   I am more discouraged than Monica.
   Mrs. Miller is the most discouraged of all.

3. A few common adjectives form irregular comparatives and superlatives.
   good, better, best
   bad, worse, worst
   many, more, most
   little, less, least

Verbs

Definition: A **verb** expresses action, either physical or mental, or it expresses a state of being.

Examples of action verbs: *sing, think, like, make, do*

Examples of verbs to express a state of being: *am, is, are, was, were, be, being, been*

Verb phrases are made up of a main verb and one or more helping or auxiliary verbs. The main verb is the last verb in the phrase. *Mr. Jones might hire me tomorrow. They could have been on vacation.*

The main auxiliary verbs are forms of *have, be, can, may, must, do, shall,* and *will*.

Forms of the verbs *do, be,* and *have* are often used as auxiliary verbs: *She has been working a lot.*

Verb tenses show different time, or tense.

Present tense:	*I look.*
Past tense:	*I looked.*
Future tense:	*I will look.*

The **present participle** is used in progressive forms to show continuing action.

Present progressive tense:	*I am looking.*
Past progressive tense:	*I was looking.*
Future progressive tense:	*I will be looking.*

The **past participle** shows finished action. It is used in the passive voice.

Present tense:	*It is being drawn.*
Past tense:	*It was drawn.*
Future tense:	*It will be drawn.*

Perfect tenses show when an ongoing action started. They consist of forms of the word and the past participle.

Present perfect tense:	*I have looked.*
Past perfect tense:	*I had looked.*
Future perfect tense:	*I will have looked.*

Principal parts of verbs are the verb, the present participle, the past and the past participle.

Regular verbs are verbs which form the past and past participle by adding *-ed*.

Present	*walk*
Present Participle (add *-ing*)	*walking*
Past (add *-ed*)	*walked*
Past participle (add *-ed*)	*walked*

Spelling rules for forming the parts of regular verbs:

1. For words ending in silent *e*, drop the *e* before adding *-ed* or *-ing*. *(live, lived, living)*

2. For words ending in a short vowel and a single consonant, double the final consonant before adding *-ed* or *-ing*. *(drop, dropped, dropping)*

Irregular verbs form the past and the past participle in a variety of ways. The present participle is formed the same as for regular verbs. See the Chart of Irregular Verbs for examples.

Contractions

Contractions are formed with nouns or pronouns and auxiliary verbs or verbs which express a state of being or having.

I am - I'm	*I will - I'll*	*is not - isn't*
you are - you're	*you will - you'll*	*are not - aren't*
he is - he's	*he will - he'll*	*was not - wasn't*
she is - she's	*she will - she'll*	*were not - weren't*
it is - it's	*it will - it'll*	*will not - won't*
we are - we're	*we will - we'll*	*would not - wouldn't*
they are - they're	*they will - they'll*	*can not - can't*
		could not - couldn't
I have - I've	*I had - I'd*	*should not - shouldn't*
you have - you've	*you had - you'd*	*has not - hasn't*
he has - he's	*he had - he'd*	*have not - haven't*
she has - she's	*she had - she'd*	*had not - hadn't*
it has - it's	*it had - it'd*	*does not - doesn't*
we have - we've	*we had - we'd*	*do not - don't*
they have - they've	*they had - they'd*	*did not - didn't*

I would - I'd
you would - you'd
he would - he'd
she would - she'd
it would - it'd
we would - we'd
they would - they'd

Chart of Irregular Verbs

Present	Past	Perfect	Present	Past	Perfect
beat	beat	beaten	let	let	let
begin	began	begun	lie	lay	lain
bend	bent	bent	lose	lost	lost
bite	bit	bitten	make	made	made
blow	blew	blown	meet	met	met
break	broke	broken	put	put	put
bring	brought	brought	raise*	raised*	raised*
build	built	built	read	read	read
burst	burst	burst	ride	rode	ridden
buy	bought	bought	ring	rang	rung
catch	caught	caught	rise	rose	risen
choose	chose	chosen	run	ran	run
come	came	come	say	said	said
cost	cost	cost	see	saw	seen
cut	cut	cut	sell	sold	sold
dig	dug	dug	set	set	set
dive	dived, dove	dived	shake	shook	shaken
do	did	done	shoot	shot	shot
drag*	dragged*	dragged*	show	showed	shown
draw	drew	drawn	shrink	shrank	shrunk
drink	drank	drunk	sing	sang	sung
drive	drove	driven	sink	sank	sunk
eat	ate	eaten	sit	sat	sat
fall	fell	fallen	sleep	slept	slept
feel	felt	felt	slide	slid	slid
fight	fought	fought	speak	spoke	spoken
fit	fit	fit	spend	spent	spent
fly	flew	flown	spread	spread	spread
forget	forgot	forgotten	spring	sprang	sprung
freeze	froze	frozen	stand	stood	stood
get	got	gotten	steal	stole	stolen
give	gave	given	sting	stung	stung
go	went	gone	swear	swore	sworn
grow	grew	grown	sweep	swept	swept
hang	hung	hung	swim	swam	swum
have	had	had	swing	swung	swung
hear	heard	heard	take	took	taken
hide	hid	hidden	teach	taught	taught
hit	hit	hit	tear	tore	torn
hold	held	held	tell	told	told
hurt	hurt	hurt	think	thought	thought
is/are	was/were	been	throw	threw	thrown
keep	kept	kept	understand	understood	understood
know	knew	known	wear	wore	worn
lay	laid	laid	win	won	won
lead	led	led	wind	wound	wound
leave	left	left	wring	wrung	wrung
lend	lent	lent	write	wrote	written

*These words are regular but are often mistaken for irregular verbs.

Adverbs

Definition: An **adverb** modifies (qualifies or limits the meaning of) a verb, adjective or another adverb. Adverbs usually tell *where, when, how,* or *to what extent.* Adverbs may consist of more than one word.

Examples: Where: *here, inside, nearby, somewhere*
When: *tomorrow, earlier, frequently, lately*
How: *quietly, quickly, well, carefully*
(Many adverbs that tell how end in *-ly*.)
To what extent (these may also be called intensifiers): *extremely, very, quite, so*

Prepositions

Definition: A **preposition** shows a relationship between a noun or a pronoun and another word in the sentence. A preposition is often more than one word.

about	*beside*	*near*
above	*besides*	*next to*
according to	*between*	*of*
across	*beyond*	*on*
after	*by*	*onto*
against	*down*	*over*
ahead of	*during*	*through*
along	*except*	*throughout*
among	*for*	*to*
around	*from*	*toward*
at	*in*	*under*
because of	*in back of*	*until*
before	*in front of*	*up*
behind	*instead of*	*with*
below	*into*	*within*
beneath	*like*	*without*

Conjunctions

Definition: Conjunctions are used to connect words, phrases or sentences: *and, but, or, however, therefore, so, if, when, except, because, though, although, unless*

Interjections

Definition: Interjections are special words which often express emotion, or serve as fillers or attention-getters. The word "interjection" comes from Latin and means "thrown in between." Most interjections are followed by commas or exclamation points.

Ouch! Whew! Oh! Hey!
Why, I know what you mean!
Well, I guess I'd better go.
Say, I have an idea.
Oh, I suppose it's all right.

Word Usage in Standard English

bring, take — *Bring* means to carry or lead someone or something **here**. *Please bring the newspaper to me.* *Take* means to carry or lead someone or something **there**. *Please take this with you to school tomorrow.*

can, may — *Can* shows the ability to do something. *She can play tennis well.* *May* asks or gives permission to do something. *May I use your telephone?*

did, done — *Did* is the past tense of *do*. *We did our work.* *Done* is used after a form of *have*. *They have done their chores. She has learned a lot.*

doesn't, don't — *Doesn't* is used with *he, she* and *it*. *Janet doesn't like ice cream.* *Don't* is used with *I, you, we* and *they*. *We don't have to leave until 9:00.*

good, well — *Good* describes something or someone. *That is a good apple.* *Well* describes an action. *He writes well.*

in, into — *In* means a location inside of something. *We drove in a car.* *Into* means motion or direction to a place within. *We drove into a car.*

lay, lie — *Lay* means to put or place something down. *Lay the books on the table, please.* *Lie* means to put or place yourself down. *I think I'll lie down and rest.*

learn, teach — *Learn* means to acquire or get knowledge. *He wants to learn French.* *Teach* means to give or impart knowledge. *The professor teaches history.*

leave, let — *Leave* means to go away. *They have to leave now.* *Let* means to permit. *He let me borrow a car.*

lend, borrow — *Lend* means to allow another person to use something of yours with the understanding that it be returned. *She will be happy to lend you a pen.* *Borrow* means to take something belonging to another person with the understanding that it will be returned. *May I borrow your hammer?*

raise, rise — *Raise* means to cause something to move upward. *It's time to raise the flag.* *Rise* means to move upward. *The sun will rise at 5:38 a.m. today.*

set, sit — *Set* means to place or put something in a certain position. *Please set the table.* *Sit* means to put yourself in a sitting position. *I will sit on the bench.*

The words listed below are those which function primarily as only *one* part of speech. Numbers indicate the first words on a list at each level.

Nouns

lot[1]	grandfather	journal
class	grandma	machine
sale	nephew	occurrence
mile	niece	privilege
size	relative	acquaintance
day	son	apology
way	uncle	appearance
week[2]	hospital	criticism
arm	prairie	summary
car	secretary	decision
hour	library	discussion
foot	article	occasion
child	character	principle
month	ridge	professor
fact	tragedy	profession
thing[3]	statement	success
year	island	conscience
teacher	argument	scene
case	author	scissors
leader	gym	
bird	action	*Proper nouns*
girl	calendar	(your city)[4]
body	direction	(your state)
moon	dollar	America
window	nickel	United States
heart	speech	Sunday
pie	ticket	Monday
breakfast	development[6]	Tuesday
dinner	example	Wednesday
road[4]	government	Thursday
death	difference	Friday
earth	magazine	Saturday
friend	opinion	January[5]
writer	neighbor	February
story	receipt	March
lesson	rhythm	April
recess	accident	May
student	disease	June
idea[5]	incident	July
noise	poem	August
office	procedure	September
period	restaurant	October
person	description	November
prison	repetition	December
captain	committee	
aunt	opportunity	
brother	system	
cousin	area	
daughter	college	

Plural nouns

men[1]
countries[4]
families
stories
parents[5]
rules
stairs
children
women

Mass nouns

art[2]
length[3]
strength
food
hair
handwriting[4]
laughter
sugar
people
trouble
beauty
happiness
clothes[5]
duty
blood
medicine
knowledge
language
money
addition
attention
excitement[6]
existence
independence
lightning
music
grammar
height
weight
relief
education
pronunciation
science

Adjectives

an	excellent[6]
a[1]	actual
hot	definite
our	immediate
your	practical
full	usual
small	convenient
my	different
nice	independent
large[2]	intelligent
their	foreign
true	weird
old	difficult
every	innocent
its	responsible
easy[3]	similar
real	national
weak	necessary
ready	brilliant
loose	familiar
afraid	conscious
main	continuous
sudden	delicious
careful[4]	humorous
wonderful	jealous
heavy	mischievous
pleasant	nervous
tough	serious
important	
terrible	**Pronouns**
happy	I
hungry	it
lucky	them[1]
sorry	him
lonely	they
beautiful	us
earlier	you
easiest	he
prettier	me
noisy[5]	she
modern	we
northern	who[2]
central	whose
able	himself
possible	itself
simple	themselves
guilty	anybody[4]
absent	everyone
interesting	somebody

Verbs

am	stayed	suppose
got[1]	told	dropped
ask	could	getting
asked	shall	grabbed
had	should	planned
has	would	planning
was	aren't	slipped
get	can't	stepped
kept	cannot	stopping
led	didn't	dining
let	doesn't	giving
went	don't	hoping
are	haven't	liked
did	weren't	lived
is	lose	making
quit	became	using
sit	become	heard[4]
win	forget	learn
gave	put	learned
give	understand	might
have	bring[3]	bought
tell	hear	brought
be	think	caught
do	eat	laughed
ate	please	taught
came	speak	write
take	teach	wrote
lay	meant	remember
may	read	carry
said	allow	carrying
say	began	hurrying
were	begin	studying
broke	choose	carried
chose	blow	hurried
come	follow	studied
been[2]	grow	entertain[5]
see	shown	destroy
seem	fail	enjoy
seen	laid	climbed
found	believe	fasten
stood	blew	listen
took	die	listened
called	died	argue
does	knew	build
filled	known	built
goes	threw	passed
looked	gotten	tying
played	happen	accept[6]
playing	happened	develop

excite	
expect	
explain	
misspell	
decieve	
receive	
seize	
continue	
describe	
identify	
imagine	
prepare	
suggest	
accommodate	
appear	
disappear	
disappoint	
embarrass	
exaggerate	
recommend	
achieve	
commit	
equipped	
occur	
occurred	
occurring	
referred	
acquaint	
apologize	
criticize	
perform	
realize	
recognize	
decide	
discuss	
possess	
succeed	
appreciate	
fascinate	

Adverbs

not	
quite[1]	
ever[2]	
never	
awhile	
why	
maybe	
really[3]	
soon	
too	
again	
anyway[4]	
everywhere	
sometimes	
instead	
already	
always	
luckily	
perhaps[5]	
certainly	
together	
often	
barely	
especially	
finally	
sincerely	
probably	
truly	
actually[6]	
carefully	
completely	
definitely	
extremely	
generally	
immediately	
practically	
usually	
accidentally	

Prepositions

at
with[1]
to
of[2]
among
from
into
upon
during[4]
toward[5]

Conjunctions

if
and[1]
than
or[2]
whether
because[4]
although
unless

Interjections

oh[2]

Word	Page	Noun	Pronoun	Adjective	Verb	Adverb	Preposition	Conjunction	Interjection
a	4			*					
a lot	52					*			
able	54			*					
about	17					2	1		
above	14					1	2		
absent	57			*					
accept	59				*				
accident	63	*							
accidentally	63					*			
accommodate	65				*				
ache	54	1			2				
achieve	66				*				
acquaint	67				*				
acquaintance	67	*							
across	46					2	1		
act	24	1			2				
action	58	*							
actual	60			*					
actually	60					*			
addition	58	*							
address	46	1			2				
affect	64	2			1				
afraid	32			*					
after	24					2	1	3	
afternoon	30	1		2					
again	32					*			
against	32						1	2	
age	11			1	2				
air	32	1		3	2				
all	9	3	2	1		4			
all right	52			2		1			
allow	29				*				
almost	46			2		1			
alone	46			1		2			
along	26					2	1		
already	46					*			
although	46							*	
always	46					*			
am	1				*				
America	40	*							
American	40	2		1					
among	20						*		
an	1			*					
and	4							*	
animal	28	1		2					
another	25		2	1					
answer	53	2			1				
any	21		2	1		3			

Word	Page	Noun	Pronoun	Adjective	Verb	Adverb	Preposition	Conjunction	Interjection
anybody	37		*						
anyway	37					*			
apologize	67				*				
apology	67	*							
appear	65				*				
appearance	67	*							
appreciate	69				*				
approach	65	2			1				
April	52	*							
arctic	55	2		1					
are	6				*				
area	66	*							
aren't	22				*				
argue	55				*				
argument	57	*							
arm	16	*							
around	17					2	1		
art	16	*							
article	54	*							
as	4		4			1	2	3	
ask	4				*				
asked	19				*				
at	1						*		
ate	11				*				
attention	58	*							
August	52	*							
aunt	50	*							
author	57	*							
away	13			2		1			
awful	38			1		2			
awhile	23					*			
back	8	1		3	2	4			
barely	55					*			
be	10				*				
bear	30	1			2				
beautiful	47			*					
beauty	45	*							
became	24				*				
because	41							*	
become	24				*				
been	15				*				
before	41					2	1	3	
began	29				*				
begin	29				*				
beginning	35	2		3	1				
being	19	2			1				
believe	33				*				
below	31					1	2		

Word	Page	Noun	Pronoun	Adjective	Verb	Adverb	Preposition	Conjunction	Interjection
benefit	61	1		2					
best	5	3		1		2			
better	34	4		1	3	2			
between	41					2	1		
bicycle	57	1		2					
big	6	3		1		2			
bird	29	*							
black	8	2		1					
blew	33				*				
blood	53	*							
blow	31				*				
blue	18	1		2					
board	38	1			2				
body	30	*							
book	18	1		3	2				
both	20		2	1		3		4	
bottom	34	1		2	3				
bought	41				*				
boy	18	1							2
bread	39	1		2					
break	34	2			1				
breakfast	34	*							
bridge	54	1			2				
brilliant	67			*					
bring	26				*				
broke	14				*				
brother	50	*							
brought	41				*				
brown	29	1		2	3				
build	56				*				
building	56	1			2				
built	56				*				
business	47	1		2					
busy	45			1	2				
but	7						2	1	
buy	40	2			1				
by	10			3		2	1		
calendar	58	*							
call	9	2			1				
called	19				*				
came	11				*				
can	4	2			1				
can't	22				*				
cannot	25				*				
captain	49	*							
car	16	*							
care	28	1			2				
careful	38			*					

Word		Noun	Pronoun	Adjective	Verb	Adverb	Preposition	Conjunction	Interjection
carefully	60					*			
carried	47				*				
carry	45				*				
carrying	46				*				
case	28	*							
catch	37	2			1				
caught	42				*				
center	38	1		3	2				
central	53			*					
certain	49	2		1					
certainly	49					*			
character	54	*							
cheat	27	2			1				
check	8	2		3	1				
chief	33	1		2					
child	20	*							
children	55	*							
chocolate	44	1		2					
choose	30				*				
chose	14				*				
circle	44	1			2				
city	45	1		2					
class	8	*							
clean	28			1	2				
clear	26			1	2	3			
climb	53	2			1				
climbed	53				*				
climbing	53			2	1				
clock	8	1			2				
close	14			1	2				
clothes	49	*							
cold	20	2		1					
college	66	*							
come	14				*				
coming	36	2			1				
commit	66				*				
committee	65	*							
complete	60			1	2				
completely	60					*			
concentrate	64	2			1				
conscience	69	*							
conscious	69			*					
continue	64				*				
continuous	69			*					
control	66	2			1				
convenient	61			*					
copy	30	1			2				
corner	38	1		2	3				

Word		Noun	Pronoun	Adjective	Verb	Adverb	Preposition	Conjunction	Interjection
cost	7	1			2				
could	21				*				
countries	47	*							
country	45	1		2					
course	42	1			2				
cousin	50	*							
cover	38	2			1				
cries	47	1			2				
criticism	67	*							
criticize	67				*				
cry	10	2			1				
crying	19			2	1				
cut	7	3		2	1				
dark	16	2		1					
daughter	50	*							
day	13	*							
dead	39	2		1		3			
dear	26	2		1					3
death	39	*							
deceive	62				*				
December	52	*							
decide	68				*				
decided	68			2	1				
decision	68	*							
deep	15	3		1		2			
definite	60			*					
definitely	60					*			
delicious	69			*					
describe	64				*				
description	64	*							
destroy	51				*				
develop	59				*				
development	59	*							
did	6				*				
didn't	22				*				
die	33				*				
died	33				*				
difference	61	*							
different	61			*					
difficult	63			*					
dining	36				*				
dinner	34	*							
direction	58	*							
dirty	29			1	2				
disappear	65				*				
disappoint	65				*				
discipline	69	1			2				
discuss	68				*				

Word		Noun	Pronoun	Adjective	Verb	Adverb	Preposition	Conjunction	Interjection
discussion	68	*							
disease	63	*							
distance	67	1		2					
do	10				*				
doctor	57	1			2				
does	19				*				
doesn't	22				*				
dog	7	1			2				
doing	19	2			1				
dollar	58	*							
don't	22				*				
done	14			1	2				
doubt	53	2			1				
down	29	5		3	4	1	2		
draw	24	2			1				
drop	7	1			2				
dropped	35				*				
dropping	35	2			1				
during	43						*		
duty	51	*							
each	27		2	1		3			
earlier	47			*					
early	39			2		1			
earth	39	*							
easiest	47			*					
east	27	1		2		3			
easy	27			*					
eat	27				*				
edge	54	1			2				
education	64	*							
effect	64	1			2				
eight	62	*							
either	62		2	1		3		4	
eleven	49	*							
else	48			1		2			
embarrass	65				*				
end	5	1		3	2				
enemy	45	1		2					
enjoy	51				*				
enough	41	2		1		3			
entertain	49				*				
equipped	66				*				
escape	63	2		3	1				
especially	55							*	
etc.	56					*			
even	18			1	2	3			
evening	18	1		2					
ever	21					*			

Word	Page	Noun	Pronoun	Adjective	Verb	Adverb	Preposition	Conjunction	Interjection
every	21			*					
everyone	37		*						
everything	37	2	1						
everywhere	37					*			
exaggerate	65				*				
example	59	*							
excellent	59			*					
except	59			2			1	3	
excite	59				*				
excitement	59	*							
exciting	59			1	2				
excuse	59	2			1				
exercise	59	1			2				
existence	61	*							
expect	59				*				
experience	59	1			2				
explain	59				*				
extremely	60					*			
eye	30	1			2				
face	11	1			2				
fact	24	*							
fail	32				*				
fair	32	2		1					
familiar	67			*					
families	47	*							
family	45	1		2					
far	16			1		2			
fascinate	69				*				
fasten	53				*				
father	50	1			2				
favorite	44	2		1					
February	52	*							
feel	15	2			1				
feeling	19	1			2				
felt	5	2		3	1				
few	33	2		1					
field	33	1		3	2				
fight	40	1			2				
figure	58	1			2				
fill	9	2			1				
filled	19				*				
final	55	2		1					
finally	55					*			
find	20	2			1				
fire	12	1			2				
first	29	3		1		2			
five	9	1		2					
fly	10	1			2				

Word	Page	Noun	Pronoun	Adjective	Verb	Adverb	Preposition	Conjunction	Interjection
follow	31				*				
food	30	*							
foot	18	*							
for	17						1	2	
force	54	1			2				
foreign	62			*					
forest	51	1		2					
forget	25				*				
forty	49	1		2					
found	17				*				
four	21	1		2					
fourth	42	2		1					
free	15			1	3	2			
Friday	43	*							
friend	41	*							
from	20						*		
front	20	1		2					
full	9			*					
further	43			1	3	2			
game	11	1		2					
gave	9				*				
generally	60					*			
get	5				*				
getting	35				*				
girl	29	*							
give	9				*				
giving	36				*				
go	10	2			1				
goes	19				*				
going	19	2		3	1				
gone	14			1	2				
good	18	2		1					3
goodbye	18	2							1
got	3				*				
gotten	34				*				
government	59	*							
grabbed	35				*				
grade	11	1			2				
grammar	62	*							
grandfather	50	*							
grandma	50	*							
gray	13	1		2	3				
great	34			1		2			
green	15	1		2	3				
ground	17	1		2	3				
group	41	1			2				
grow	31				*				
guarantee	63	1			2				

Word	Page	Noun	Pronoun	Adjective	Verb	Adverb	Preposition	Conjunction	Interjection
guard	56	2			1				
guess	56	2			1				
guilty	56			*					
gym	57	*							
had	4				*				
hair	32	*							
half	53	1		2		3			
hand	4	1			2				
handwriting	42	*							
happen	34				*				
happened	34				*				
happiness	47	*							
happy	45			*					
hard	16			1		2			
has	4				*				
have	9				*				
haven't	22				*				
he	10		*						
head	39	1		2	3				
hear	26				*				
heard	39				*				
heart	33	*							
heavy	39			*					
height	62	*							
hello	18	2							1
help	5	2			1				
her	16		1	2					
here	13	2				1			3
high	40	3		1		2			
him	6		*						
himself	25		*						
his	6		2	1					
home	14	1		2	3				
hope	14	1			2				
hoping	36				*				
hopping	35			2	1				
horse	17	1		3	2				
hospital	51	*							
hot	7			*					
hour	17	*							
house	17	1			2				
how	29					1		2	
however	29					2		1	
humorous	69			*					
hundred	49	1		2					
hungry	45			*					
hurried	47				*				
hurry	45	2			1				

Word		Noun	Pronoun	Adjective	Verb	Adverb	Preposition	Conjunction	Interjection
hurrying	46				*				
hurt	43	2			1				
I	2		*						
I'll	22								
I'm	22								
idea	48	*							
identify	64				*				
if	2							*	
imagine	64				*				
immediate	60			*					
immediately	60					*			
important	44			*					
impossible	54	2		1					
in	2					2	1		
incident	63	*							
independence	61	*							
independent	61			*					
innocent	63			*					
inside	25	1		2		3	4		
instead	39					*			
intelligent	61			*					
interest	57	1			2				
interesting	57			*					
into	25						*		
is	6				*				
island	56	*							
it	2		*						
it's	22								
its	22			*					
itself	25		*						
January	52	*							
jealous	69			*					
journal	66	*							
July	52	*							
June	52	*							
just	7			2		1			
keep	15	2			1				
kept	5				*				
key	56	1		2					
kind	20	2		1					
knew	33				*				
know	31	2			1				
knowledge	54	*							
known	31				*				
laid	32				*				
language	56	*							
large	16			*					
last	4	3		1	4	2			

Word		Noun	Pronoun	Adjective	Verb	Adverb	Preposition	Conjunction	Interjection
later	38			1		2			
laugh	42	2			1				
laughed	42				*				
laughter	42	*							
lay	13				*				
lead	28	2		3	1				
leader	28	*							
learn	39				*				
learned	39				*				
least	27	2		1		3			
leave	27	2			1				
led	5				*				
leisure	62	1		2					
length	26	*							
less	8	2		1		3			
lesson	46	*							
let	5				*				
let's	22								
library	52	*							
lie	33	1			2				
life	12	1		2					
light	40	1		2	3				
lightning	61	*							
like	12	3		2			1	4	
liked	36				*				
line	12	1			2				
list	6	1			2				
listen	53				*				
listened	53				*				
little	37	2		1					
live	9			2	1	3			
lived	36				*				
living	36	2		1	3				
lonely	46			*					
long	26	3		1	4	2			
look	18	2			1				
looked	19				*				
loose	30			*					
lose	23				*				
lot	7	*							
love	14	1			2				
low	31	3		1		2			
luck	8	1			2				
luckily	47					*			
lucky	45			*					
machine	66	*							
made	11			2	1				
magazine	61	*							

Word		Noun	Pronoun	Adjective	Verb	Adverb	Preposition	Conjunction	Interjection
main	32			*					
make	11	2			1				
making	36				*				
man	4	1		2					3
many	21	2		1					
March	52	*							
matter	34	1			2				
may	13				*				
May	52	*							
maybe	25					*			
me	10		*						
mean	28			2	1				
meant	28				*				
measure	39	2			1				
medicine	53	*							
meet	15	2			1				
men	5	*							
middle	44	1		2					
might	40				*				
mile	12	*							
million	49	1		2					
mind	20	1			2				
minute	51	1		2					
mischievous	69			*					
miss	8	2			1				
misspell	61				*				
modern	51			*					
Monday	43	*							
money	56	*							
month	20	*							
moon	30	*							
more	23	2		1		3			
morning	18	1		2					
most	20	2		1		3			
mother	50	1		3	2				
motor	57	1		2					
mountain	49	1		2					
move	9	2			1				
moving	36			1	2				
Mr.	40								
Ms.	40								
much	7	2		1		3			
music	61	*							
must	7	2			1				
my	10			*					
name	11	1			2				
national	64			*					
near	26			2	4	1	3		

Word	Noun	Pronoun	Adjective	Verb	Adverb	Preposition	Conjunction	Interjection
necessary 65			*					
need 15	2			1				
neighbor 62	*							
neither 62			3		2		1	
nephew 50	*							
nervous 69			*					
never 21					*			
new 33	3		1		2			
next 5			1		2			
nice 12			*					
nickel 58	*							
niece 50	*							
night 40	1		2					
nine 12	1		2					
nineteen 49	1		2					
ninety 49	1		2					
no 10			2		1			
nobody 37	2	1						
noise 48	*							
noisy 48			*					
north 17	1		2		3			
northern 51			*					
not 3					*			
note 14	1			2				
nothing 37	1			2				
notice 48	1			2				
November 52	*							
now 29	2				1		3	4
occasion 68	*							
occur 66				*				
occurred 66				*				
occurrence 66	*							
occurring 66				*				
October 52	*							
of 17						*		
off 8			3		1	2		
office 48	*							
often 53					*			
oh 17								*
old 20			*					
on 3			3		2	1		
once 21	2				1		3	
one 14	1	3	2					
only 24			1		2			
open 24	2		1	3				
opinion 61	*							
opportunity 65	*							
opposite 65	2		1		4	3		
or 17							*	
other 20		2	1					
our 8			*					
out 17			2		1	3		
outside 25	1		2		3			
over 24			3		2	1		
own 31	3		2	1				
page 11	1			2				
paid 32	2			1				
parallel 65	2		1	3				
parents 50	*							
part 16	1		3	2				
particular 63	2		1					
pass 8	2			1				
passed 57				*				
patient 61	2		1					
pattern 51	1			2				
pay 13	2		3	1				
peculiar 67	2		1					
people 44	*							
perfect 48			1	2				
perform 67				*				
perhaps 48					*			
period 48	*							
person 48	*							
physical 68	2		1					
picture 58	1			2				
pie 33	*							
piece 33	1			2				
place 11	1			2				
plain 32	3		1		2			
plan 4	1			2				
planned 35				*				
planning 35				*				
play 13	1			2				
played 19				*				
playing 19				*				
pleasant 39			*					
please 27				*				
pocket 58	1		3	2				
poem 63	*							
point 48	1			2				
poison 48	1		3	2				
poor 53	2		1					
possess 68				*				
possible 54			*					
power 29	1		2	3				
practical 60			*					
practically 60					*			
practice 48	1			2				
prairie 51	*							
prepare 64				*				
prettier 47			*					
pretty 45			1		2			
price 12	1			2				
principal 68	2		1					
principle 68	*							
prison 48	*							
private 41	2		1					
privilege 66	*							
probably 56					*			
problem 44	1		2					
procedure 63	*							
profession 68	*							
professor 68	*							
program 44	1			2				
progress 68	1			2				
promise 44	1			2				
pronunciation 64	*							
purpose 43	1			2				
put 25				*				
question 58	1			2				
quick 8			1		2			
quiet 34			1	2				
quit 6				*				
quite 12					*			
rain 32	1			2				
raise 32	2			1				
reach 27	2			1				
read 28				*				
ready 28			*					
real 27			*					
realize 67				*				
really 27					*			
reason 28	1			2				
receipt 62	*							
receive 62				*				
recess 46	*							
recognize 67				*				
recommend 65				*				
red 5	1		2					
reference 61	1		2					
referred 66				*				
regular 58	2		1					
relative 50	*							
relief 66	*							

Word	#	Noun	Pronoun	Adjective	Verb	Adverb	Preposition	Conjunction	Interjection
remember	44				*				
repeat	64	2		3	1				
repetition	64	*							
responsible	63			*					
restaurant	63	*							
return	43	2		3	1				
rhythm	62	*							
ridge	54	*							
right	40	3		1	4	2			
road	38	*							
room	30	1			2				
rules	51	*							
run	7	2			1				
running	35	1		2					
safety	55	1		2					
said	13				*				
sale	11	*							
same	11		2	1		3			
sandwich	65	1			2				
Saturday	43	*							
saw	24	1			2				
say	13				*				
scare	28	2			1				
scared	36			1	2.				
scene	69	*							
school	30	1		3	2				
science	69	*							
scissors	69	*							
sea	28	1		2					
search	39	2			1				
season	28	1			2				
second	20	2		1	4	3			
secret	51	2		1					
secretary	51	*							
see	15				*				
seem	15				*				
seen	15				*				
seize	62				*				
sense	58	1			2				
sentence	53	1			2				
separate	63			2	1				
September	52	*							
serious	69			*					
seven	21	2		1					
several	56	2		1					
shall	21				*				
she	10		*						
shine	12	2			1				

Word	#	Noun	Pronoun	Adjective	Verb	Adverb	Preposition	Conjunction	Interjection
shining	36			2	1				
short	17			1		2			
should	21				*				
show	31	2		3	1				
shown	31				*				
sick	8	2		1					
side	12	1		2					
sign	56	1			2				
similar	63			*					
simple	54			*					
since	55					3	1	2	
sincerely	55				*				
single	44	2		1	3				
sister	50	1		2					
sit	6				*				
six	21	1		2					
size	12	*							
skiing	57	2			1				
sledding	35	2			1				
sleep	15	2			1				
slipped	35				*				
slow	31			1	3	2			
small	9			*					
smile	12	2			1				
smooth	30			1	3	2			
so	10					1		2	3
social	55	2		1					
some	14		2	1					
somebody	37		*						
something	37	1				2			
sometimes	37					*			
somewhere	37	2				1			
son	50	*							
soon	30					*			
sorry	45			*					
south	17	1		2		3			
speak	27				*				
special	55	2		1					
speech	58	*							
spring	26	2		3	1				
stairs	51	*							
stand	4	2			1				
start	16	2			1				
state	11	1		2	3				
statement	55	*							
stay	13	2			1				
stayed	19				*				
stepped	35				*				

Word	#	Noun	Pronoun	Adjective	Verb	Adverb	Preposition	Conjunction	Interjection
still	9	2		1	3	4		5	
stomach	54	1		2					
stood	18				*				
stop	7	2			1				
stopped	35			2	1				
stopping	35				*				
stories	47	*							
story	45	*							
straight	57			1		2			
street	15	1		2					
strength	26	*							
stretch	37	2		3	1				
strong	26			1		2			
student	46	*							
studied	47				*				
study	45	1			2				
studying	46				*				
succeed	68				*				
success	68	*							
such	7			1		2			
sudden	34			*					
sugar	43	*							
suggest	64				*				
summary	67	*							
summer	34	1		2					
Sunday	43	*							
suppose	34				*				
supposed to	34								
sure	43	3		1		2			
surprise	44	1		3	2				
surprised	44			2	1				
swimming	35	1		3	2				
system	65	*							
table	54	1		2	3				
take	11				*				
taking	36	2			1				
talk	16	2			1				
taught	42				*				
teach	27				*				
teacher	27	*							
team	28	1		3	2				
tell	9				*				
terrible	44			*					
than	4							*	
thank you	26								
that	4		2	1		4		3	
that's	22								
the	6								

word		Noun	Pronoun	Adjective	Verb	Adverb	Preposition	Conjunction	Interjection
their	18			*					
them	5		*						
themselves	25		*						
then	5	2				1			
there	13	2				1			
these	13		2	1					
they	6		*						
they're	22								
thing	26	*							
think	26				*				
third	29	2		1					
this	6		2	1		3			
those	14		2	1					
though	41					2		1	
thought	41	1			2				
thousand	49	1		2					
three	15	1		2					
threw	33				*				
through	41			3		2	1		
throw	31	2			1				
Thursday	43	*							
ticket	58	*							
tie	57	2			1				
tight	40			1		2			
time	12	1			2				
tired	36			1	2				
to	10						*		
today	25	1				2			
together	51					*			
told	20				*				
tomorrow	31	1				2			
too	30					*			
took	18				*				
touch	41	2			1				
tough	41			*					
toward	56						*		
town	29	1		2					
tragedy	54	*							
tried	47			1	2				
trouble	44	*							
true	18			*					
truly	57					*			
try	10	2			1				
trying	19			1	2				
Tuesday	43	*							
turn	43	2			1				
twelve	49	1		2					
twenty-one	49	1		2					

word		Noun	Pronoun	Adjective	Verb	Adverb	Preposition	Conjunction	Interjection
two	21	1		2					
tying	57				*				
type	38	1			2				
uncle	50	*							
under	24					2	1		
understand	25				*				
United States	40	*							
unless	46							*	
until	38						1	2	
up	7			3		1	2		
upon	25						*		
us	7		*						
use	14	2			1				
used to	36								
using	36				*				
usual	60			*					
usually	60					*			
very	21			2		1			
view	33	1			2				
voice	48	1			2				
wait	32	2			1				
waiting	32			2	1				
walk	16	2			1				
want	16	2			1				
war	16	1			2				
warm	16			1	3	2			
was	4				*				
watch	37	2			1				
water	38	1		3	2				
way	13	*							
we	10		*						
weak	27			*					
wear	30	2			1				
weather	39	1			2				
Wednesday	43	*							
week	15	*							
weight	62	*							
weird	62			*					
welcome	24	2		3	1				4
well	9	3				1			2
went	5				*				
were	13				*				
weren't	22				*				
what	23		1	2		3			4
when	23	4	3			1		2	
where	23	4	3			1		2	
whether	23							*	
which	23		1	2					

word		Noun	Pronoun	Adjective	Verb	Adverb	Preposition	Conjunction	Interjection
while	23	1						2	
white	23	2		1					
who	23		*						
who's	23								
whole	23	2		1					
whose	23		*						
why	23					*			
wide	12			1		2			
will	9	2			1				
win	6				*				
window	31	*							
winter	38	1		2	3				
wish	6	2			1				
with	6						*		
without	25						2	1	
woman	55	1		2					
women	55	*							
wonder	38	1			2				
wonderful	38			*					
word	24	1			2				
work	24	1		2	3				
world	24	1		2					
would	21				*				
wreck	42	1			2				
write	42				*				
writer	42	*							
writing	42	2		3	1				
written	42			2	1				
wrong	42	2		1					
wrote	42				*				
year	26	*							
yellow	31	1		2					
yes	5	2						1	
yesterday	38	1						2	
you	8		*						
you're	22								
young	41	2		1					
your	8			*					
(your city)	40	*							
(your state)	40	*							

Definite article: the

Indefinite articles: a, an

WORD HISTORIES

This section is included for your reference as you teach the *Spelling Plus* 1000 word list. As I studied English spelling, I was fascinated with the stories behind some of our words and their spellings. Many of the spellings students "invent" were once acceptable, even preferred. Except for accidents of history, those spellings might be correct today. The selections below illustrate the development of English spelling.

This section contains historical information on the words in the *Spelling Plus* core list. If students become interested in etymology, check the library for books about word histories.

Depending on the level you teach, you may wish to give students an overview of the history of the English language, using *Spelling Plus* pp. 4–7 as a source of information. This can be tied into a long time line on permanent display in the classroom. Mine extends from 3000 B.C. to 2000+ A.D., and is marked off in 100 year increments, labeled every 500 years (3000 B.C., 2500 B.C., and so on).

Time Line of World History
Ancient Egypt, 3000 B.C. to 715 B.C.
　Picture of Great Sphinx or Pyramids
Ancient Greece, 800 B.C. to 300 B.C.
　Picture of the Parthenon
Ancient Rome, 500 B.C. to 455 A.D.
　Picture of the Roman Colosseum
Birth of Christ, c. 1 A.D.
　Picture of nativity scene
Middle Ages, 476 A.D. to 1450 A.D.
　Pictures of castles
Columbus, 1492 A.D.
　Picture of Columbus' ships
U.S.A. began, 1776 A.D.
　Picture of Liberty Bell or U.S. flag

If you or your students are interested, consider doing a unit on Greek and Latin word roots and word-building. Put the roots (p. 78), as well as prefixes and suffixes (pp. 56–57), on small cards and have students combine them to form words. Write these new words along with their probable definitions. Use the dictionary to see which of the words is actually listed.

From Beowulf, in Old English, c.700 A.D.
　þā wæs Bīowulfe　brōga gecȳðed
snūde tō sōðe,　þæt his sylfes hām,
bolda sēlest,　bryne-wylmum mealt,
gif-stōl Gēata.　Þæt ðām gōdan wæs
hrēow on hreðre,　hyge-sorga mæst.
Wēnde se wīsa,　þæt hē Wealdende
ofer ealde riht,　ēcean Dryhtne,
bitre gebulge;　brēost innan wēoll
þēostrum geþoncum,　swā him geþȳwe ne wæs.

Translation of Beowulf
So times were pleasant for the people there
until finally one, a field out of hell,
began to work his evil in the world.
Grendel was the name of this grim demon
haunting the marches, marauding round the heath
and the desolate fens; he had dwelt for a time
in misery among the banished monsters,
Cain's clan, whom the Creator had outlawed
and condemned as outcasts for the killing of Abel.

From The Canterbury Tales, by Chaucer, c.1400
　Selection from The Knightes Tale
And weddede the quene Ipolita,
And broghte hir hoom with him in his contree
With muchel glorie and greet solempnitee,
And eek hir yonge suster Emelye.
And thus with victorie and with melodye
Lete I this noble duk to Athenes ryde,
And al his hoost, in armes, him bisyde.

From Romeo and Juliet, by Shakespeare, 1597
IULIET
　Go get thee hence, for I will not away.
　Whats heere? a cup closd in my true loues hand?
　Poison I see hath bin his timelesse end:
　O churle, drunke all, and left no friendly drop
　To help me after, I will kisse thy lips,
　Happlie some poyson yet doth hang on them,
　To make me dye with a restoratiue.
　She kisses Romeos lips

GREEK AND LATIN WORD ROOTS

Word roots from Greek and Latin are helpful in figuring out the meanings of unfamiliar words. Experts estimate that about 60% of common English words come from Latin or Greek.

Root	Meaning	Examples	Root	Meaning	Examples
-aqua-	water	aquarium	-pel-	drive	compel, repel, expel
-audi-	hear	audience, audition	-pend-	hang	depend, pendulum
-biblio-	book	bibliography	-phil-	love	philosophy
-cede-	go	recede, precede	-phobia-	fear	claustrophobia
-ceed-	go	exceed, proceed	-phon-	sound	phonics, telephone
-cept-	take	intercept, reception	-phot-	light	photography
-chrom-	color	monochrome	-phys-	nature	physics, physical
-chron-	time	chronic, synchronize	-plex-	network	complex, perplex
-cide-	kill	suicide, decide	-pod-	foot	tripod, podiatrist
-clud-	close	seclude, include	-port-	carry	portable, transport
-cred-	believe	incredible, credit	-poten-	power	potent, potential
-dent-	tooth	indent, dentist	-press-	press	impress, depress
-derm-	skin	epidermis	-psych-	mind	psychology, psychic
-dict-	say	dictator, contradict	-rupt-	break	disrupt, interrupt
-duct-	lead	conduct, product	-scien-	knowledge	science, conscience
-fide-	faith	fidelity, confidence	-scend-	climb, go	ascend, descent
-flamm-	fire	flammable	-scop-	see, look	microscope, telescope
-flex-	bend	flexible, reflex	-scri-	write	describe, prescription
-flor-	flower	florist, florid	-sect-	cut	dissect, intersection
-flu-	flow	fluent, influence	-serv-	protect	conserve, observe
-gramm-	letter	telegram, grammar	-spect-	look, see	inspect, spectator
-graph-	writing	autograph, telegraph	-stell-	star	constellation
-gress-	walk	progress, congress	-stig-	goad, prick	instigate, stigma
-homo-	alike	homonym	-struct-	build	construct, structure
-ject-	throw	eject, reject, inject	-tact-	touch	intact, tactile
-jour-	day	journey, adjourn	-tain-	hold	maintain, retain
-junct-	join	junction, conjunction	-tend-	stretch, pull	pretend, tendency
-leg-	law	legal, legislature	-therap-	treatment	psychotherapy
-loc-	place	locate, locus	-therm-	heat	thermometer, thermal
-man-	hand	manufacture, manual	-tim-	fear	timid, intimidate
-miss-	send	missionary, dismiss	-tort-	twist	distort, torture, extort
-mit-	send	transmit, admit	-tract-	draw, pull	tractor, subtract
-mort-	death	mortal, mortician	-ven-	come	convention, intervene
-nov-	new	novice, novelty	-vert-	turn	convert, divert
-pan-	all	panacea, panorama	-vis-	see	visible, supervise
-pan-	bread	pantry, company	-vit-	life	vitality, vitamin
-path-	suffering	sympathy, pathology	-viv-	alive	survive, revive
-ped-	foot	pedal, pedestrian	-voc-	voice	vocal, vocation

a   **article**

a Reduced form of *an*, used since 1200 before a word beginning with a consonant. At one time, *in* was reduced to *i* and *on* to *o*.

able Old French 1400.

about Old English.

above Middle English spellings progressed from *abufan* to *abuve* to *above*. For legibility in handwritten manuscripts, Norman scribes often used *o* rather than *u* before *v*.

absent Old French 1400, ultimately from *ab* (away) + *esse* (be).

accept Old French 1400, ultimately from *ad* (motion to or toward) + *cept* (take).

accident Old French 1400, ultimately from *ad* (motion to or toward) + *cadere* (fall).

accidentally *See accident.*

accommodate Latin 1400, first used by Shakespeare, from *ad* (motion to or toward) + *com* (together, with) + *modus* (measure).

ache Old English. In 1820 *ake* was an acceptable spelling.

achieve Old French 1400, ultimately from *ad* (motion to or toward) + *chief* (head), and meaning "coming or bringing to a head, or end."

acquaint Old French 1800, ultimately from *ad* (motion to or toward) + *cognitus* (know).

acquaintance *See acquaint*

across Old French 1300 *a croix*. Acceptable spellings in 1500 included *acros, acrosse*.

act Latin 1400.

action Old French 1400.

actual Old French 1400.

actually *See actual.*

addition Latin 1500, ultimately from *ad* (motion to or toward) + *dare* (put).

address Old French 1400, ultimately from *ad* (motion to or toward) + *directum* (straight, direct). This word had one **d** in French. The spelling was changed upon adoption into English to reflect the Latin roots and another *d* was added.

affect French or Latin 1700, ultimately from *ad* (motion to or toward) + *facere* (do).

afraid Middle English, replacing the Old English word *affeared*. *Afraid* was once the past participle of the verb *affray* which meant "alarm, startle, frighten." Acceptable spellings in Middle English included *affraied* and *afrayed*. At one time, the past participle of the verb *stay* was *staid*. This remains the case with *paid*.

after Old English.

afternoon 1800, from *after* + *noon*.

again Old English.

against Old English, once spelled *agains*.

age Old French 1300.

air Old French 1300.

all Old English.

all right *See all and right.*

allow Old French 1400, ultimately from *ad* (motion to or toward) + *laudare* (praise).

almost Old English, from *all* + *most*, originally meaning "most all."

alone Old English, from *all* + *one*.

along Old English, spelling progressed from *andlong* to *anlong* to *allong* to *along*.

already From *all* + *ready*.

although From *all* + *though*, originally *though all*.

always Old English, from *all* + *way*.

am Old English.

America Latin 1507, from Amerigo Vespucci, an explorer who claimed to have explored what is now the American mainland in 1497. A German mapmaker who believed this claim suggested that the new land be named *America*. The claim proved to be false.

among Old English, from words meaning "on" + "mingling."

an Old English, reduced form of *one*, unstressed.

and Old English.

animal Old French 1600, from the same root as *animate*, meaning "breath, soul, spirit."

another 1600 *an* + *other*, written as two words in Middle English.

answer Old English, ultimately from *anti* (against) + *swear*. Originally meant a solemn statement made to rebut a charge.

any Old English. In Middle English, this word was spelled in two ways, *ani* and *eni*. We currently spell this word after the first *(ani)* and pronounce it after the second *(eni)*.

anybody 1800 *any* + *body*.

anyway From *any* + *way*.

apologize *See apology.*

apology French 1800, ultimately from *apo* (return) + *log* (speak).

appear Old French 1400, ultimately from *ad* (motion to or toward) + *parere* (come into view).

appearance *See appear.*

appreciate Latin or French 1700, ultimately from *ad* (motion to or toward) + *propius* (nearer).

April Latin 1400, from *Aprilis*, derived from a word meaning "to open."

arctic Old French 1400, ultimately from Greek *arktos*, meaning "bear." The connection between *arctic*, which pertains to the north, and *bear* is the Big Dipper and Little Dipper, also called *Ursa Major* and *Ursa Minor*, meaning "big bear" and "little bear." *Arctic* was once spelled *artik* or *artic* but was refashioned after the Latin *arcticus* in the 1700s.

are A form of the verb *be*. *Are* is from German, of unknown origin.

area Latin 1600.

aren't *See are and not.*

argue Old French 1400, with the original meaning "debate, discuss, prove."

argument *See argue.*

arm Old English.

around Old French 1400 *à la reonde* later *a* + *round*.

art Old French 1300, ultimately from *ar* (fit, join).

article Old French 1300, ultimately from *ar* (fit, join).

as Old English, from the same word as *also*.

ask Old English, spelled as *ask* from 1200.

asked *See ask*.

at Old English, spelled variously in Middle English as *atten, atte, ate, atter*.

ate This spelling is from one of the Middle English spellings for *at*. The pronunciation *et* was associated with the spelling *ate*.

attention Old French 1300, ultimately from *ad* (motion to or toward) + *tendere* (stretch). *Attend* and *attendance* are from the same source.

August Old English *August* from Latin *Augustus,* named after the first Roman emperor, Augustus Caesar.

aunt Anglo Norman 1300, spelled *ante* in Old French.

author Anglo Norman 1400, spelled *autor* in Old French and *autour* in Middle English. The spelling was Latinized in 1500 to *auctour* or *auctor* and progressed to *aucthor, authour* and finally *author*. The *th* influenced the pronunciation. Ultimately from *auct* (increase, promote, originate). *Authority* and *authorize* are from the same source.

away Old English, originally *on way*.

awful Old Norse 1300, from *awe* (dread) + *ful* (full of).

awhile Old English *one hwile*, later *a + while*. Norman scribes changed the *hw* to *wh*.

back Old English.

barely Old English.

be Old English.

bear Old English.

beautiful *See beauty*.

beauty Anglo Norman 1300, spelled *bealte, beute,* and *beaute* in Middle English.

became *See become*.

because Middle English 1400 *bi cause*, from *bi* (by) + *cause* (after), after Old French *par cause de*, meaning "by reason of."

become Old English.

been *See be*.

before Old English *beforan*.

began *See begin*.

begin Old English.

beginning *See begin*.

being *See be*.

believe Old English.

below From *by + low*.

benefit Anglo Norman *benfet,* ultimately from *bene* (well) + *facere* (do). The Middle English spelling was *benfet*. The first syllable changed to *bene* to reflect Latin in 1500, and *fet* changed to *fit* in 1600.

best Old English.

better Old English, originally *bet,* changed to *better* in 1700.

between Old English, ultimately from *be* (by), *tweon* (two).

bicycle French 1900, from *bi* (two) + *kuklos* (circle, wheel).

big 1600, unknown origin.

bird Old English *brid,* superseding *fowl*. The variation *bird* is from Northumbrian dialect.

black Old English *blac*. The name of this color was formerly *swart*.

blew *See blow*.

blood Old English.

blow Old English.

blue Old French 1300, spelled *bleu* or *blew* in Middle English.

board Old English *bord*.

body Old English.

book Old English *boc,* usually thought to be a derivative of *boka* (beech), the wood of the tree being the material of tablets upon which runes were inscribed.

both Old Norse 1200.

bottom Old English *botm*.

bought *See buy*.

boy Old French 1400, ultimately from a root meaning "fetters." The original meaning was "man in fetters, slave."

bread Old English *bread,* pronounced with a long **e**. The vowel was shortened as in *breath, dead, lead, read, thread* and *threat*.

break Old English *brecan*.

breakfast 1400, from the phrase *break one's fast*.

bridge Old English.

brilliant French 1800, from French *briller* (shine).

bring Old English *bringan,* past tense *brohte*. Norman scribes changed *ht* to *ght*.

broke *See break*.

brother Old English.

brought *See bring*.

brown Old English *brun,* related to the word *bruin* (bear).

build Old English *byldan*. The spelling reflects a southern and western development *(ui),* the pronunciation is northern and midland.

built *See build*.

business Old English from *busy + ness*. This word was spelled *buisness* by Dryden in 1697.

busy Old English *bisig*. The spelling reflects a southern and western development *(u),* the pronunciation is northern and midland.

but Old English.

by Old English.

buy Old English. In the north, this word was spelled *bi* before 1300. The current spelling reflects a southern and western development *(u),* the pronunciation is northern and midland.

calendar Anglo Norman 1300. Spelled *kalender* in Middle English. The spelling was changed to reflect the Latin *calendarium*.

call Old English.

called *See call*.

came *See come*.

can Old English, with the primary meaning "have learned, come to know."

can't *See can and not*.

cannot *See can and not*.

captain Old French 1400, ultimately from *caput* (head). The Middle English spelling was *capitain*.

car   daughter

car Anglo Norman 1400, spelled *carre* in Middle English, related to Latin *currus* (chariot).

care Old English.

careful *See* **care**.

carefully *See* **care**.

carried *See* **carry**.

carry Anglo Norman 1400, related to Latin *currus* (chariot).

carrying *See* **carry**.

case Old French 1400, ultimately from *cadere* (fall).

catch Anglo Norman 1300, from *cachier* (to hunt). *Catch* took over the sense "seize" and its conjugational forms such as *caught* from the English word *latch*.

caught *See* **catch**. Although this past tense form was taken from the English word *latch*, the past tense of *latch*, which was once *laught*, is now *latched*.

center Old French or Latin 1400. From 1400 to 1700, the prevalent spelling was *center*. Samuel Johnson chose the spelling *centre*, which is how the word is still spelled in England, Canada, and other countries formerly part of the British Commonwealth of Nations.

central From *center* 1600.

certain Old French 1300.

certainly *See* **certain**.

character Old French 1500, ultimately from a Greek word meaning "scratch, engrave." Spelled *caracter* in Middle English, but changed to reflect Latin *character*.

cheat Anglo Norman 1400.

check Old French 1400, originally from Persian and referring to a chess game.

chief Old French 1300, from *chef*, ultimately from *caput* (head).

child Old English, a word peculiar to English, with no cognates in any other language. Spelled *childre* in Middle English.

children *See* **child**. The **-en** suffix to pluralize was once common in English but is now restricted to *children, oxen* and *brethren*.

chocolate French, Spanish, Aztec 1700.

choose Old English. Spelled *chuse* between 1400 and 1800. Samuel Johnson changed it to *choose* in his dictionary.

chose *See* **choose**.

circle Old French 1400. Spelled *cercle* in Middle English, but changed to reflect Latin *circulus*.

city Old French 1300. A more dignified substitute for Old English *burh* (borough). Spelled *cite* in Middle English.

class Latin 1700, originally one of the six ancient divisions of the Roman people.

clean Old English.

clear Old French 1300. Spelled *cler* in Middle English.

climb Old English *climban,* with the original sense being "hold fast, cleave, cling." In Scottish, the original conjugation is preserved: *clim, clam, clum*.

climbed *See* **climb**.

climbing *See* **climb**.

clock German 1400, introduced by Flemish clockmakers brought to England by Edward I.

close Old French 1300.

clothes Old English. Spelled *cloaths* or *close* in Middle English.

cold Old English *cald*.

college Old French or Latin 1400.

come Old English *cuman*. Norman scribes changed the *u* to *o* for legibility next to *m, n, u, v,* or *w*.

coming *See* **come**.

commit Latin 1400, from *com* (together) + *mit* (put, send).

committee Latin 1700.

complete Old French or Latin 1400, ultimately from *com* (together) + *ple* (full).

completely *See* **complete**.

concentrate Latin 1700, from *con* (together) + *centrum* (center), and having the meaning "bring to a common center."

conscience Old French 1300, ultimately from *con* (together) + *sci* (know).

conscious Latin, from same base as *conscience*.

continue Old French 1400.

continuous *See* **continue**. 1700.

control Anglo Norman 1500, ultimately from *contra* (against) + *rotulus* (roll), with the meaning "exercise restraint over."

convenient Latin 1500, from *con* (together) + *venire* (come).

copy Old French 1400.

corner Anglo Norman 1300. The meaning "to drive into a corner" originated in the U.S. in the 1900s.

cost Anglo Norman 1300, ultimately from *com* (together) + *stare* (stand), meaning "to stand firm, be fixed, stand at a price."

could *See* **can**. This word was spelled *coude* in Middle English. The spelling was changed to be consistent with *should* and *would*.

countries *See* **country**.

country Old French 1300. Spelled *cuntre* or *contre* in Middle English.

course Old French 1300, ultimately from *currere* (run).

cousin Old French 1300. Spelled *cusin* or *cosin* in Old French, currently *cousin* in French.

cover Old French 1300, ultimately from *con* (completely) + *operire* (over).

cries *See* **cry**.

criticism *See* **criticize**.

criticize Latin 1600, ultimately from Greek *kritikós,* related to *crisis*.

cry Old French 1300, ultimately from Latin *quiritare*, a word which came from calling upon the *Quirites* (Roman citizens) for help.

crying *See* **cry**.

cut Old English.

dark Old English.

daughter Old English *dohtor* or *doughter*. This word has no cognates in other languages. Scottish *dauchter* and northern English *dowter*. The standard pronunciation is of dialectical origin. In early Modern English the word was pronounced *dafter*.

day Old English.

dead Old English.

dear Old English.

death Old English.

deceive Old French 1300, ultimately from *de* (away) + *capere* (take). The Latin base was *deceptus*. At one time a *p* was inserted into *deceit* but that spelling didn't survive as it did with *receipt*.

December Old French 1300, ultimately from *decem* (ten). December was the tenth month of the ancient Roman year. In 46 B.C., Julius Caesar changed the calendar to begin the year on January 1 rather than March 1.

decide French or Latin 1400, ultimately from *de* (away) + *caedere* (cut, kill).

decided *See decide.*

decision *See decide.* 1500.

deep Old English. The Middle English comparative was *depper* (now *deeper*).

definite Old French 1500, ultimately from *de* (away) + *finir* (finish).

definitely *See definite.*

delicious Old French 1300, ultimately from *de* (away) + *lacere* (deceive), with an original sense of "luring away."

describe Latin 1500, ultimately from *de* (down) + *scribere* (write).

description *See describe.*

destroy Old French 1300, ultimately from *de* (down) + *struere* (build).

develop Old French 1600, ultimately from *dis* (opposite) + *volup* (wrap). Spelled *disvelop* in Middle English. The sense is "unfold, lay open." It is the opposite of *envelop*.

development *See develop.*

did *See do.*

didn't *See did and not.*

die Old English or Old Norse (disputed). *Dead* is an older word.

died *See die.*

difference *See different.*

different Old French 1400, ultimately from *dis* (apart) + *ferre* (carry).

difficult Back-formed from *difficulty* which came from French or Latin 1500, ultimately from *dis* (opposite of) + *facilis* (easy).

dining Old French 1300, ultimately from *dis* (opposite of) + *jejunare* (fast).

dinner *See dining.* This word was spelled *diner* in Middle English.

direction Latin 1400, ultimately from *de* (down) + *regere* (put straight, rule). This word is related in origin to *address*.

dirty Old Norse 1300. Spelled *drit* in Middle English. The current spelling first appears in 1500.

disappear *See appear.*

disappoint Old French 1500, ultimately from *dis* (opposite of) + *appoint* (to a point).

discipline Old French 1300, ultimately from *discere* (learn).

discuss Latin 1500, ultimately from *dis* (apart) + *qatere* (shake) with the primary meaning "dash to pieces, disperse, dispel."

discussion *See discuss.*

disease Anglo Norman 1400, from *dis* (opposite of) + *ease.*

distance Old French 1500, ultimately from *dis* (apart) + *stare* (stand).

do Old English.

doctor Old French 1400, ultimately from *docere* (teach).

does *See do.* Spelled *dos* or *dus* in Middle English.

doesn't *See does and not.*

dog Late Old English *docga*. This replaced the older word *hund* (hound). Similar animal names were *frocga* (frog), *picga* (pig), and *stacga* (stag).

doing *See do.*

dollar Early Flemish 1600, from Low German *daler*, German *taler* which was short for *Joachimstaler*, a silver coin which could be obtained in Joachimstal (Joachim's valley) in Erzgebirge, Germany.

don't *See do and not.*

done *See do.*

doubt Old French 1300. This word was once spelled *doute*. The spelling was changed to reflect the Latin word *dubitare* in 1500.

down Old English.

draw Old English.

drop Old English.

dropped *See drop.*

dropping *See drop.*

during Old French 1400, ultimately from *durare* (harden, endure).

duty Anglo Norman 1300, from *due* (owe) + *-ty* (state or condition of).

each Old English.

earlier *See early.*

early Old English from *ere* (before) + *-ly.*

earth Old English. Interestingly, the Middle English spelling for *earthquake* was *erthdin.*

easiest *See easy.*

easy Anglo Norman 1200, from *ease* + *y.*

east Old English.

eat Old English *etan.*

edge Old English.

education Latin 1500, from *educare,* ultimately from *ex* (going out) + *ducere* (lead). Closely related to the word *educe,* with the primary meaning of developing from a latent condition.

effect Old French or Latin 1400, ultimately from *ex* (going out) + *facere* (make, do).

eight Old English *ehta.*

either Old English. The *ei* was once pronounced as in *neighbor.*

eleven Old English.

else Old English.

embarrass French 1700.

end Old English.

enemy Old French 1300, ultimately from *in* (not) + *amicus* (friend).

enjoy Old French 1400, from *en* (put into) + *joy.*

enough Old English. The plural *enow* was used until 1800.

entertain Old French 1500, from *inter* (among) + *tenere* (hold).

equipped French 1600.

escape

escape Anglo Norman 1400, once spelled *ascape*. Ultimately from *ex* (going out) + *cuppa* (cloak).

especially Old French 1600. The word *special* was once written as *especial*, and is from the same root as *species*.

etc. Old English from Latin, abbreviation for *et* (and) + *cetera* (the rest).

even Old English.

evening Old English, from a word meaning "grow towards night."

ever Old English.

every Old English, from same origin as *each*.

exaggerate Latin 1700, from *ex* (going out) + *aggerare* (heap up).

example Old French 1400, ultimately from *ex* (out) + *emere* (take).

excellent Latin 1500, from *ex* (out) + *cellere* (rise high, tower).

except Old French 1400, ultimately from *ex* (out) + *capere* (take).

excite Old French or Latin 1400 from *ex* (out) + *citare* (set in motion).

excuse Old French 1300, ultimately from *ex* (out) + *causa* (accusation). Sometimes spelled *escuse* in Middle English.

exercise Old French 1600, ultimately from *ex* (out) + *arcere* (shut up, keep off, restrain, prevent).

existence Latin 1700, from *ex* (out) + *sistere* (take up a position).

expect Latin 1600, from *ex* (out) + *spectare* (look).

experience Old French 1400, ultimately from *ex* (out) + *periculum* (experiment, risk). The words *expert, experiment* and *peril* are from the same root.

explain Latin 1500, from *ex* (out) + *planus* (flat).

extremely Old French 1500, related to *supreme*.

eye Old English.

face Old French 1300.

fact Latin 1600 *factum,* from *facere* (do).

fail Old French 1300.

fair Old English.

familiar Latin 1500, from *familia* (household).

families *See* **family**.

family Latin 1500, from *familia* (household).

far Old English.

fascinate Latin 1600, from *fascinum* (spell, witchcraft).

fasten Old English.

father Old English *faeder.* The *d* was changed to *th* as in *mother, brother, together,* etc.

favorite French 1600, spelled *favourite* in England.

February Old French 1300, from *februarius*, a Roman festival of purification held on February 15. Once spelled *feverer,* but changed to reflect Latin spelling.

feel Old English.

few Old English.

field Old English *feld.*

fight Old English *feohte.*

figure Old French 1300.

fill Old English.

final Old French or Latin 1400, from *finis* (end).

find Old English.

fire Old English.

first Old English.

five Old English *fif.*

fly Old English.

follow Old English.

food Old English.

foot Old English.

for Old English.

force Old French 1300, ultimately from *fortis* (strong).

foreign Old French 1300, ultimately from *fores* (out of doors), spelled *forein* until about 1400.

forest Old French 1300, ultimately from *fores* (out of doors). The Anglo Norman word is *foster,* now used as a surname.

forget Old English, with the primary meaning "miss, lose one's hold."

forty Old English, spelled *fourty* until about 1750.

found *See* **find**. In Middle English, *fond* or *foond* was used, later changed to conform to the past tense of *bind, grind, wind.*

grammar

four Old English.

free Old English, with the primary sense of "dear," applied to members of the family of the head of house as opposed to slaves.

Friday Old English for *Frigg's Day,* after the Norse goddess of love.

friend Old English. Originally *friend* was the plural, *freond* was singular. The spellings *frend, freind* and *freend* were used in Middle English. The word *fiend* is similar, but preserves the long vowel. The vowel sound was shortened in *friend,* perhaps due to compounds such as *friendship.*

from Old English.

front Old French 1300.

full Old English.

further Old English.

game Old English *gamen,* later changed as did *maid,* from *maiden.*

gave *See* **give**.

general Old French 1300, ultimately from *genus* as opposed to *species, general* as opposed to *special.*

get Old Norse 1300. The past participle *gotten* was used before 1400 and is still used in the U.S.

girl Probably Old English, spelled *gurle, girle* or *gerle* in Middle English.

give Old English, spelled *yive, yeve, yaf* or *yeven* in Middle English. The *g* replaced *y* due to the Scandinavian *giva.*

go Old English.

good Old English.

goodbye Contraction of the phrase "God be with ye," with *good* later substituted for *God* after *good day* and *good night.*

government Old French 1400, ultimately from Greek *kubernân* (steer).

grabbed Middle Dutch or Middle Low German 1600.

grade Latin 1600, from *gradus* (step).

grammar Anglo Norman 1400, ultimately from Greek *gramatike* (pertaining to letters).

grandfather

just

grandfather French 1600.
gray Old English.
great Old English.
green Old English *grene*.
ground Old English *grund*.
group French 1700.
grow Old English.
guarantee Spanish or French 1700, earlier spelled *garante*, from same base as *warrant*.
guard Old French 1600, once spelled *gard*, related to *ward* as in *warden*.
guess perhaps Middle Low German 1300, spelled *gesse* in Middle English. The spelling with *gu* dates from 1600.
guilty Old English.
gym Latin 1600, ultimately from Greek *gumnásion* (train, literally train in the nude).

hair Old English.
half Old English.
hand Old English.
handwriting 1600 from *hand* + *writing*.
happen Old Norse 1300, from *happ* (chance, good luck).
happy Old Norse 1300, from *happ* (chance, good luck).
hard Old English.
have Old English.
he Old English.
head Old English.
hear Old English.
heart Old English.
heavy Old English.
height Old English, spelled *hight* in Middle English, the present spelling represents an older pronunciation with *ei*.
hello Charles Dickens 1900, spelled variously *hallo, hello, hillo* and *hullo* in 1900s.
help Old English, with the original past tense *halp*.
her Old English, spelled *hir* in Middle English.
here Old English, spelling changed to match *there*.
high Old English, originally pronounced like *hee* but vowel sound raised as in *die*.

him Old English.
his Old English.
home Old English.
hope Old English.
hopping Old English.
horse Old English *hors*.
hospital Old French 1300, ultimately from *hospitium* (hospitality), related to the words *hostel* and *hotel*.
hot Old English.
hour Anglo Norman 1300, ultimately from Greek *hora*. Spelled *ure* or *oure* in Middle English. The *h* was added to reflect the Greek. The *h* has not influenced the pronunciation as it has in the words *humble* and *humor*.
house Old English, once spelled *hus*.
how Old English.
humorous Anglo Norman 1400, once spelled either with or without the *h*.
hundred Old English. The pronunciation *hunderd* was once considered proper.
hungry Old English.
hurry 1600, origin unknown, may relate to Middle High German *hurren* (move quickly).
hurt Old French 1200, variously *hürte, hirte, herte* in Middle English.

I Old English *ic*, becoming *i* in a stressed position in 1200. Some dialects still use *ich*. The capitalization was initiated by scribes. In handwritten manuscripts, a small *i* was likely to be lost or attached to another word. A capital *I* helped keep this a distinct, separate word.
idea Latin 1600, from Greek *idea* (ideal form, model).
identify Late Latin 1700, from *edem* (same).
if Old English.
imagine Old French 1300, ultimately from *imaginare* (form an image of).
immediate Old French or late Latin 1600.
important Latin 1500.

impossible Old French 1300, from *im* (not) + *posse* (be) + *ible* (capable of), recorded in English before *possible*.
in Old English. *In* was reduced to *i* before a consonant before 1200, as it still is in some dialects. *See a.*
incident French or Latin 1500, ultimately from *in* (towards) + *cadere* (fall).
independent French 1700, ultimately from the root *pend* (hang).
innocent Old French 1400, ultimately from *in* (not) + *nocere* (hurt, injure).
inside 1400, compound *in* + *side*.
instead Old English, originally two words *in stead*, with the word *stead* meaning "place" as in *homestead*.
intelligent Old French or Latin 1600, ultimately from *inter* (between) + *legere* (pick up, gather, read).
interest Old French 1500, probably from *inter* (between) + *esse* (be), originally spelled *interesse*.
into Written as two words until 1600.
is Old English form of *to be*.
island Old English, once spelled *iland*. The spelling was changed in the 1600s to assimilate to *isle*.
it Old English *hit*, spelled *it* in unstressed positions by 1200.

January Latin 1400, ultimately from *Janus*, an ancient Italian deity with two faces, one looking forward and the other looking backward
jealous Old French 1300, ultimately from Greek *zêlos* (zeal).
journal Old French 1400, ultimately from *diurnalis* (occurring daily).
July Anglo Norman *julie* 1300, named after *Julius* Caesar, who was born in this month. The name of the month was changed from *Quintilis* after Caesar's death. The stress has shifted from the first to the second syllable since 1750.
June Old French 1300, after *Juno*, the goddess of marriage.
just Old French 1400.

keep

music

keep Late Old English *cepan*.

key Old English. Pronounced to rhyme with *they* until 1700.

kind Old English *cynd*.

knew Late Old English *cneow*.

know Late Old English *cnawan*.

knowledge 1300, spelled *cnouleche* in Middle English.

laid *See* **lay**.

language Old French 1300, spelled *langage* (later *language*) in Middle English, ultimately from *lingua* (tongue, language).

large Old French 1200, ultimately from *larga* (abundant).

last Old English, originally the superlative form of *late*.

later Old English *latter*. *Later* and *latest* are new formations.

laugh Old English.

laughter Old English.

lay Old English.

lead Old English, first appeared in northern dialects, later called a "low, despicable word."

leader Old English.

learn Old English.

least Old English, from *less* + *est*.

leave Old English.

leisure Anglo Norman 1400.

length Old English, usually spelled *lengu* until 1700s.

less Old English.

lesson Old French 1300.

let Old English. Related to Latin *lassus* (weary). The primary sense was probably "let go through weariness."

library Old French 1400, ultimately from *liber* (book) + *ary* (pertaining to).

lie Old English.

life Old English.

light Old English.

lightning 1400, specialized use of *lightening*.

like Old English.

line Old English.

list Old English, but the current meaning of a catalog of names, etc. is from French.

listen Old English from *hlyst* (hearing).

little Old English.

live Old English *libban*.

lonely *See* **alone**.

long Old English.

look Old English.

loose Old Norse 1300, spelled *los* in Middle English.

lose Old English, once pronounced with a long *o* as in *chose*.

lot Old English *hlot*, referring to a game of chance. The meaning "large number" is from 1900s.

love Old English *lufu*. The *u* was changed to *o* by Norman scribes for legibility in handwritten manuscripts next to the letter *v*.

low Old Norse 1200.

luck Low German 1500, probably originally a gambling term.

machine Old French 1600.

main Old English.

make Old English, spelled *macan* or *macen* in Middle English.

man Old English. This word meant "human being" in Old English, as the cognates still do in German and Dutch. Words showing gender were *werman* (man) and *wifman* (woman).

many Old English. The old pronunciation was as in *manifold*. Changed on analogy with *ani / eni*. *See* **any**.

March Old French 1200, ultimately from Mars, the Roman god of war.

matter Anglo Norman 1300, ultimately from a Greek word meaning the substance of which the *mater* (mother) consists.

may Old English.

May Old French, from *Maia*, the Roman goddess of spring and growth.

maybe 1500 from *may* + *be*.

me Old English.

mean Old English.

meant *See* **mean**.

measure Old French 1300, spelled *mesur* in Middle English.

medicine Old French 1300.

meet Old English.

men *See* **man**.

middle Old English *middel*.

might Old English.

mile Old English, originally a Roman measure of 1,000 paces.

million Old French 1400.

mind Old English.

minute Old French 1400, ultimately from Latin *pars minuta prima* (first minute part), meaning 1/60 of a unit in the Babylonian system of fractions. Applied by Ptolemy in A.D. 11 to the degrees of the circle, the application to the division of the hour came later.

mischievous Anglo Norman 1400, ultimately from *mis* (bad) + *chevar* (come to a head, happen).

miss Old English.

misspell From *mis* (bad) + *spell*.

modern Old French 1600, ultimately from *modo* (just now).

Monday Old English, from *moon* + *day*.

money Old French 1300, variously spelled *money, moneie* and *mone* in Middle English.

month Old English.

moon Old English.

more Old English.

morning Old English *morgen*. Spelled *morwen, morun, moren, morn, morwe* and *moru*. Changed to *morning* in 1300, after *evening*.

most Old English.

mother Old English *modor*.

motor Latin 1600, ultimately from *movere* (move), not applied to machines before 1900.

mountain Old French 1300.

move Anglo Norman 1300.

Mr. Old English. A weakened form of *master*. Abbreviation appeared in 1600.

Ms. Recent title for women which circumvents the problem of whether to address a woman as *Miss* or *Mrs*.

much Old English.

music Old French 1300, ultimately from the Greek word for Muse, one of nine goddesses of the arts and sciences in Greek mythology. They had pleasing, melodic voices and often sang in a chorus.

must   perfect

must Old English.

my Reduced form of *mine* used before a consonant, as *my son* but *mine eyes.*

name Old English.

national Old French 1600, ultimately from *nat* (born).

near Old Norse or the comparative form of Old English *nigh.*

necessary Anglo Norman or Latin, ultimately from *esse* (be) + *ary* (pertaining to).

need Old English.

neighbor Old English from *na* (near) + *búa* (dwell). Spelled *neighbour* in England.

neither Old English from *no whether,* spelled after *either.*

nephew Old French 1300. Spelled *neveu* in Middle English.

nervous Latin 1600.

never Old English from *ne* (not) + *ever.*

new Old English.

next Old English superlative of *nigh.*

nice Old French 1300. The meaning in French was "silly, simple," in Latin it was "ignorant." Ultimately from *ne* (not) + *scire* (know). The meaning "agreeable, delightful" came in the 1800s.

nickel Named in 1754 by Swedish mineralogist Axel F. von Cronstedt, shortening of *kupfernickel* (copper nickel), the mining name of the ore from which the metal was first obtained in 1751. The element *nickel* means "dwarf, mischievous demon," the name given to the ore because it yielded no copper despite its promising appearance.

niece Old French 1300.

night Old English *niht.*

nine Old English.

nineteen *See* **nine**.

ninety *See* **nine**.

no Old English.

nobody Originally written as two words.

noise Old French 1400, ultimately from *nausea* (sea-sickness).

north Old English.

not Reduced form of *nought.*

nothing Originally written as two words.

notice Old French 1500, not commonly used before mid-1800s, mentioned by Benjamin Franklin in 1789 as a recently current word.

November Old French 1300, ultimately from *novem* (nine). November was the ninth month of the year until Julius Caesar changed the calendar in 46 B.C., making January the first month of the year rather than March.

now Old English.

occasion Old French or Latin 1400, ultimately from *ob* (towards) + *cadere* (fall).

occur Latin 1600, from *ob* (towards) + *currere* (run).

occurrence *See* **occur**. This word was once spelled *occurrents.*

October Late Old English from Latin *octo* (eight). October was the eighth month of the year until Julius Casear changed the calendar in 46 B.C., making January rather than March the first month of the year.

of Old English.

off Once a variation of *of,* not differentiated in use until 1600s.

office Old French 1300, ultimately from *opus* (work) + *facere* (do).

often Old English.

oh French or Latin.

old Old English.

on Old English.

once Old English. Spelled *anes* or *ones* in Middle English, and pronounced with a long *o.* The pronunciation with *w* is of westerly origin where it was spelled *wonus.*

one Old English. Originally pronounced with a long *o.* The *w* is of westerly origin where they also say *woak* for *oak.*

only Old English, from *one* + *ly.*

open Old English, from *up.*

opinion Old French 1300.

opportunity Old French 1400, ultimately from *ob* (towards) + *portus* (harbor). *Portunus* was a god that protected harbors.

opposite Old French 1400, ultimately from *ob* (against) + *poner* (place).

or First appeared in 1200.

other Old English, with an original sense of alternation.

our Old English.

out Old English.

outside From *out* + *side.*

over Old English. Spelled *ouere* or *uuere* in 1300. Later *v* replaced *u.*

own Old English, not used between 1400 and 1600 except as *owner,* but revived in 1700s.

page Old French 1500.

paid *See* **pay**.

parallel French 1600, ultimately from Greek *para* (alongside).

parents Old French 1500, ultimately from *parere* (bring forth).

part Old French 1300.

particular Old French 1400. Spelled *particuler* in Middle English, later changed to reflect Latin *particularis.*

pass Old French 1300, ultimately from *passus* (step).

patient Old French 1400, ultimately from *pati* (suffer).

pattern Old French 1600, from *patron* in Middle English. The sense is from the idea of a patron giving an example to be copied.

pay Old French 1200, ultimately from *pac* (peace). The sense is from the idea of pacifying a creditor.

peculiar Latin 1500, from *peculium* (private property, esp. cattle).

people Anglo Norman 1300. Spelled *peple, poeple* or *people* in Middle English. Ultimately from *populus* (people).

perfect Old French 1300, ultimately from *per* (completely) + *facere* (make). Spelled *parfit* or *parfet* in Middle English. Spelling changed to reflect Latin *perfectus.*

perform   recess

perform Anglo Norman 1400, ultimately from *per* (completely) + *fournir* (furnish).

perhaps Middle English compound of *per* + *haps* (chance, good luck).

period Old French 1400, ultimately from Greek *periodos* (circuit, revolution).

person Old French 1300, ultimately from Greek *prosopon* (face, mask, dramatic part).

physical Old French 1500, ultimately from Greek *phusis* (nature). Spelled *fisikal* in Middle English, but changed to reflect Greek roots.

picture Latin 1500, from *pict* (paint, embroider).

pie Old French 1400, ultimately from *magpie*. The sense may be from the idea that a magpie collects miscellaneous objects.

piece Anglo Norman 1300. Spelled *pece* as well as *piece* in Middle English.

place Old French 1300, ultimately from Greek *plateîa* (broad way). This word replaced the Old English word *stead*.

plain Old French 1300, ultimately from *planus* (flat). Not differentiated from *plane* until 1700s.

plan French 1800.

play Old English.

pleasant Old French 1400, from same root as *please*.

please Old French 1400, ultimately from *placare* (placate). Spelled *plaise* or *plese* in Middle English.

pocket Anglo Norman 1500.

poem Old French or Latin 1600, ultimately from Greek *poesis* (creation, poetry).

point Old French 1400, ultimately from *pungere* (prick, pierce).

poison Old French 1400, from *potion* which comes from *potare* (drink). Spelled *puison* or *poison* in Middle English.

poor Old French 1300, ultimately from *pauper*. Spelled *povere, pouere, poure,* or *pore* in Middle English.

possess Old French 1500, ultimately from *potis* (power) + *sidere* (sit).

possible Old French or Latin 1400, from *posse* (be). *Impossible* came into English earlier.

power Anglo Norman 1300, ultimately from *potere* (be able). Spelled *poer* or *pouer* in Middle English.

practical French 1700, ultimately from Greek *praktikós* (practice).

practice Old French 1600, ultimately from Greek *praktikós* (practice).

prairie French 1800, ultimately from *pratum* (meadow).

prepare French or Latin 1500, from *pre* (before) + *parare* (make ready).

prettier *See* **pretty**.

pretty Old English. The original meaning was "crafty, wily."

price Old French 1300, from *pretium* (price, value, wages, reward). Spelled *pris, priis, prise* and finally *price* in Middle English.

principal Old French 1300, ultimately from *princeps* (prince) + *al* (pertaining to).

principle Anglo Norman 1400, from Latin *principium* (beginning, source).

prison Old French 1200.

private Latin 1400, from *privus* (single, individual, private).

privilege Anglo Norman 1200, ultimately from *privus* (private) + *leg* (law).

probably Old French 1400, ultimately from *probare* (prove). Original sense was *provable, credible*.

problem Old French 1400, ultimately from Greek *pro* (before) + *bállein* (throw).

procedure Old French 1400, from *proceed* (spelled *procede* in Middle English), ultimately from *pro* (before) + *cedere* (go).

profession Old French 1400, ultimately from *pro* (before) + *fateri* (confess). In Latin, *profiteri* meant "declare aloud or publicly."

professor 1900, from *profess*. *See* **profession**.

program Latin 1700, ultimately from Greek *pro* (before) + *graphein* (write).

progress Latin 1500, from *pro* (before) + *gradi* (step, walk, go).

promise Latin 1400, from *pro* (before) + *mittere* (send).

pronunciation Old French 1500, from *pronounce,* ultimately from *pro* (before) + *nuntiare* (announce).

purpose Old French 1300.

put Old English.

question Old French 1300, ultimately from *quaerere* (seek, inquire).

quick Old English *cwic*. Norman scribes changed *cw* to *qu*.

quiet Anglo Norman 1400, ultimately from *quietus* (be quiescent, motionless, at rest).

quit Old French 1300, ultimately from *quietus* (quiet).

quite Old French 1400, originally a form of *quit*.

rain Old English.

raise Old Norse 1200, correlated to Old English *rear*.

reach Old English.

read Old English. The past tense of this verb was once spelled *rad* or *red,* but since 1700 the infinitive, past, and participle have been identical in spelling. The pronunciation is on the analogy of *lead*.

real Anglo Norman 1500, ultimately from *res* (thing) + *al* (pertaining to).

reason Old French 1300, ultimately from *ratio* (reckoning, account, judgment). Spelled *resun, reson,* or *reisun* in Middle English.

receipt Anglo Norman 1400. Spelled *receit* in Middle English, but changed to reflect Latin *recepta*.

receive Old French 1300, ultimately from *re* (back) + *capere* (take). Spelled *receive* or *receve* in Middle English.

recess Latin 1600 from *re* (back) + *cedere* (go), meaning "go back, recede."

recognize Latin 1500 from *re* (again) + *cognoscere* (get to know, investigate).

recommend Latin 1700, from *re* (with force) + *commendare* (commend, praise).

red Old English *read.* The vowel was shortened as in *bread, dead* and *lead,* but in this case, the spelling changed to reflect the pronunciation. The long *e* is still heard in the surnames *Read, Reid* and *Rede,* meaning "red."

reference Old French 1600, ultimately from *re* (back) + *ferre* (carry, bear).

regular Old French 1600, ultimately from *regula* (rule).

relative Old French or Latin 1600, base word is *relate.*

relief Anglo Norman 1400, ultimately from *re* (again) + *levare* (raise).

remember Old French 1400, ultimately from *re* (again) + *memor* (mindful).

repeat Old French 1400, ultimately from *re* (again) + *petere* (lay claim to, ask). Spelled *repete* in Middle English.

responsible Old French 1600. A *response* is an *answer, responsible* means *answerable.*

restaurant French 1900, from *restore.*

return Old French 1400, from *re* (back) + *turn.*

rhythm Latin or French 1600, ultimately from Greek *rhuthmós,* related to *rheîn* (flow).

ridge Old English, originally meaning "back, spine."

right Old English *riht.* The *ht* once stood for a guttural sound. Norman scribes changed *ht* to *ght.*

road Old English.

room Old English.

rules Old French 1300 from Latin *regula.* Spelled *riule* or *reule* in Middle English.

run Old English. Spelled *rinne* or *renne* in Middle English.

safety Old French 1300, spelled *sauvete* in Middle English (3 syllables).

sale Old English.

same Old Norse 1200.

sandwich 1800. This item was invented for John Montagu, 11th earl of Sandwich (1718-1792) so that he might not leave the gaming-table, at which he spent 24 hours without other refreshment.

Saturday Old English from Latin, Saturn's Day.

saw Old English.

say Old English.

scare Old Norse 1200. Spelled *skerre, scarre* or *skere, skayre, skare* and finally *scare* in Middle English.

scene Latin 1800, ultimately from Greek *skene* (tent, booth, stage, scene).

school Old English.

science Old French 1400, ultimately from *scire* (know).

scissors Old French 1400, ultimately from *cidere* (cut). The spelling with *sc* dates from 1600 and is due to association with Latin *scindere* (carve). This was not the correct root for the word.

sea Old English.

search Anglo Norman 1400, ultimately from *circare* (go round).

season Old French 1300, ultimately from *satus* (sown). Spelled *seson, sesun,* or *sesoun* in Middle English.

second Old French 1300, ultimately from *sequi* (follow). In Old English, there was no good ordinal number with this meaning. *Other* was used (as in "every other day") but was ambiguous. The application to time comes from Latin *secunda minuta* (second minute), a mathematical term.

secret Old French 1400, ultimately from *se* (apart) + *cernere* (separate, distinguish, secrete).

secretary Late Latin 1400, from *secret* (see above) + *ary* (pertaining to).

see Old English.

seem Old Norse 1200. Spelled *seme* in Middle English.

seize Old French 1300.

sense Latin 1400, from *sentire* (feel).

sentence Old French 1300, ultimately from *sentire* (feel) through Latin *sententia* (mental feeling, opinion, judgment).

separate Old French 1500, ultimately from *se* (apart) + *parare* (make ready).

September Latin, ultimately from *septem* (seven). September was the seventh month until Julius Caesar changed the calendar in 46 B.C., making January rather than March the first month of the year.

serious Old French 1500.

seven Old English.

several Anglo Norman 1500, from *sever,* ultimately from *separare* (separate).

shall Old English.

she A new form in east midlands Middle English because Old English *he* (he) and *heo* (she) had converged.

shine Old English.

short Old English.

should Old English.

show Old English. The meaning of this word changed from *see* to *cause to be seen.* Other languages retain the first meaning.

sick Old English. This word once rhymed with *like* and was spelled *sek, syke* and later *sikel, sickel* in Middle English.

side Old English.

sign Old French 1300, ultimately from *signum* (signal).

similar French or Latin 1700.

simple Old French 1300.

since Old English. Spelled *synnes* or *syns* in Middle English.

sincerely Latin 1600.

single Old French 1400. Spelled *sengle* in Middle English.

sister Old Norse 1300.

sit Old English.

six Old English.

size   tomorrow

size Old French 1300.

skiing Norwegian 1900.

sledding Middle Low German 1400.

sleep Old English.

slipped Middle Low German 1300.

slow Old English.

small Old English.

smile Swedish or Danish 1300.

smooth Old English.

so Old English.

social French or Latin 1600, ultimately from *sociare* (unite). Rousseau's essay "Le contrat social" (1762) popularized the meaning "pertaining to human society."

some Old English *sum*. Norman scribes changed *u* to *o* before *m* for legibility in handwritten manuscripts.

somebody Middle English compound 1400.

son Old English *sunu*. Norman scribes changed *u* to *o* before *m* for legibility in handwritten manuscripts.

soon Old English.

sorry Old English. Spelled *sory* in Middle English, but in the 1700s spelling changed to assimilate to *sorrow*, an unrelated word.

south Old English, meaning "sun side."

speak Old English.

special Old French or Latin, ultimately from *species + al* (pertaining to).

speech Old English.

spring Old English.

stairs Old English.

stand Old English.

start Old English. Spelled *sterte* or *starte* in Middle English.

state Latin 1300.

statement 1800.

stay Old English.

stepped Old English.

still Old English.

stomach Old French 1400, ultimately from Greek *stómakhos* from *stóma* (mouth). Spelled *stomak* in Middle English, but changed to reflect Latin *stomachus*.

stop Old English.

story Anglo Norman 1300, ultimately from Latin *historia*.

straight Once the past participle of *stretch,* which meant "make straight."

street Old English.

strength Old English, from *strong + th*.

stretch Old English.

strong Old English.

student Latin 1500, from *studere* (be eager or diligent, study).

study Old French 1300, originally from Latin *studium* (zeal, affection, painstaking application).

succeed Old French or Latin 1500, ultimately from *sub* (near) + *cedere* (go).

success Latin 1600.

such Old English.

sudden Anglo Norman 1300, ultimately from *sub* (secretly) + *ire* (go). Spelled *soden, sodein* or *sodain* in Middle English.

sugar Old French 1300, ultimately from Arabic. The spelling development in Middle English is: *suker, sucre, sugre, suger* and finally *sugar* in 1600.

suggest Latin 1600, ultimately from *sub* (up) + *gerere* (bring).

summary Old French 1500, ultimately from *summa* (sum) + *ary* (pertaining to).

Sunday Old English "day of the sun."

suppose Old French 1400, ultimately from *sub* (up) + *poser* (pose).

sure Old French 1400, from Latin *securus* (secure).

surprise Old French 1500, ultimately from *sur* (above) + *praehendere* (seize).

swim Old English.

system French or Latin 1700, ultimately from Greek *sustema* (an organized whole).

table Old French 1200, from Latin *tabula* (plank or tablet).

take Old English.

talk Middle English *talken,* from the base of *tale*.

taught *See* **teach**. There were two past tense forms in Middle English, *teched* and *tahte*.

teach Old English.

team Old English.

tell Old English.

terrible Old French, ultimately from *terrere* (frighten).

than Old English, not differentiated from *then* until 1700s. In Dutch, *dan* still has both meanings.

thank Old English.

that Old English.

the Middle English, superseded all cases from Old English.

their Old Norse 1200.

them Old Norse.

then from *than,* differentiated in 1700s.

there Old English.

these Middle English development 1300.

they Old Norse 1200.

thing Old English.

think Old English.

third Old English. Spelled *thrid* in Middle English and Scottish until 1800. *Thirteen* was spelled *threeten* as late as the 1700s.

this Old English.

those Old English.

though Old Norse 1200.

thought Old English.

thousand Old English, meaning "many hundreds."

three Old English.

threw *See* **throw**.

Thursday Old English "Thor's Day" named for the god of thunder.

ticket French 1600 *étiquet*. This word also became the English *etiquette* but the primary sense is that of *ticket*.

tie Old English.

tight Old English and Old Norse.

time Old English and Old Norse.

tired Old English.

to Old English.

today Old English.

together Old English. Spelled *togedere* in Middle English.

told *See* **tell**.

tomorrow Old English.

too a stressed form of *to,* spelled with two *o's* since 1600s.

took *See* **take**.

touch Old French 1300. Spelled *toche, tuche* or *touche* in Middle English.

tough Old English.

toward Old English, from *to* + *ward* (direction).

town Old English.

tragedy Old French 1400, possibly from Greek *trágos* (goat) + *oide* (ode).

tried *See* **try**.

trouble Old French 1300, ultimately from Latin *turbidus* (turbid).

true Old English. Spelled *trewe, truwe,* or *tru* in Middle English. The spelling *true* dates from 1500.

try Old French 1300.

turn Old English. Spelled *turne* or *terne* in Middle English.

twelve Old English.

twenty-one Old English.

two Old English *twa*.

tying *See* **tie**.

type French or Latin 1500, ultimately from Greek *túptein* (strike, beat).

uncle Anglo Norman 1300.

under Old English.

understand Old English.

United States *Unite* is from Latin *unire* (join together).

unless Late Middle English, from *on less* patterned after Old French *à moins que*. Joined to form *onless,* but lack of stress and negative implication led to *un*.

until Old Norse 1300, from *und* + *till*.

up Old English.

upon 1200, from *up* + *on*.

us Old English. Spelled *ous* or *ows* in Middle English with a long vowel, stressed. The unstressed variation *us* led to our current spelling.

use Old French 1300. Spelled *us* in Middle English.

usual Old French 1400, ultimately from *usus* (use) + *al* (pertaining to).

very Old French 1300, ultimately from *verus* (true). Spelled *verray* in Middle English.

view Anglo Norman 1500, ultimately from *videre* (see).

voice Anglo Norman 1300, ultimately from *vox* (voice).

wait Old Norman French 1200.

walk Old English *wealcan*.

want Old Norse 1200.

war Anglo Norman 1200. *Werre* was a Norman variation of *guerre*.

warm Old English.

was Part of the verb *to be,* from Old English infinitive *wesan,* meaning "dwell, remain."

watch Old English.

water Old English.

way Old English.

we Old English.

weak Old Norse 1300.

wear Old English.

weather Old English *weder*.

week Old English.

weight Old English. Spelled *wiht, wight,* then *weght, weiht,* or *weight* in Middle English.

weird Old English. Spelled *wird* in Middle English; the present form depends on dialectical variations *wirid, weirid, werd, weird*. This word became popular after being used by Shakespeare in *MacBeth*.

welcome 1200, combination of *well* + *come*.

well Old English.

went Originally past tense of *wend;* past tense for *go* since 1500.

were Part of the verb *to be,* from Old English infinitive *wesan,* meaning "dwell, remain."

what Old English *hwaet*. Norman scribes changed *hw* to *wh*.

when Old English *hwenne*. Norman scribes changed *hw* to *wh*. Spelled *whon* till 1500, *whan* till 1600.

where Old English *hwaer*.

whether Old English.

which Old English *hwilc*.

while Old English *hwil*.

white Old English *hwit*.

who Old English *hwa*. Spelled *hoo* 1300–1500, *hwo* 1700–1800, and *who* since 1800.

whole Old English, from the same base as *heal*. The spelling is due to a widespread dialectical pronunciation with *w* appearing in 1600.

whose Old English. Spelled *hwos* from 1700-1800.

why Old English *hwi* or *hwy*.

wide Old English.

will Old English.

window Old Norse 1300 from *vindr* (wind) + *auga* (eye).

winter Old English, generally used to mean "year."

wish Old English.

with Old English.

without Old English.

woman Old English *wifman*. From *wif* (woman) + *man* (human being). Older words were *wif* (now *wife*) and *cwene* (now *queen*). The sound *wim* was changed to *wum* and then *wom* in the 1800s.

wonder Old English. Norman scribes changed *u* to *o* for legibility in handwritten manuscripts.

wonderful *See* **wonder**.

word Old English.

work Old English. Once spelled *wirch* but influenced by Old Norse and *k* prevailed in 1500.

world Old English.

would Old English.

wreck Anglo Norman from Old Norse 1300.

write Old English.

wrong Late Old English.

wrote Old English.

year Old English.

yellow Old English, related to *jealous*.

yes Old English from *gia sie* (yea, may it be so).

yesterday Old English.

you Plural of *thou*. Began to be used in 1500 for *ye* and in 1400s as a substitute for *thee* and *thou* in respectful address to a superior.

young Old English.

your Old English.

Check the web site: www.SusanCAnthony.com for current prices and editions as well as sample activities, workshop handouts, and much more. Order online!

	Quantity	Extended Cost

Materials to Help Students Learn Spelling

Spelling Plus: 1000 Words Toward Spelling Success* Item 048 $19.95 _____ _____
Dictation Resource Book for use with *Spelling Plus* Item 137 $12.95 _____ _____
Homophones Resource Book* Item 145 $15.95 _____ _____
Personal Dictionary* Item 153 $3.50 _____ _____
Spell Well: A One-Year Review for Older Students Item 042 $11.95 _____ _____

Materials to Help Students Learn Handwriting

Manuscript Handwriting Masters* Item 161 $8.50 _____ _____
Cursive Handwriting Masters* Item 17X $10.50 _____ _____

Materials to Help Students Learn Reference Skills

Facts Plus: An Almanac of Essential Information, 250 pages
   Item 196, $19.95 _____ _____
   Item 19D, $14.96 each for orders of 25 or more almanacs. _____ _____
Facts Plus Activity Book* 182 pages
   Item 110 $24.95 _____ _____
Encyclopedia Activity for use with *The World Book Encyclopedia**
   Item 129 $9.50 _____ _____

Materials to Help Students Learn Math

Addition Facts in Five Minutes a Day* Item 056 $11.95 _____ _____
Subtraction Facts in Five Minutes a Day* Item 064 $11.95 _____ _____
Multiplication Facts in Five Minutes a Day* Item 072 $13.95 _____ _____
Division Facts in Five Minutes a Day* Item 080 $11.95 _____ _____
Casting 9's: A Quick Check for Math Computation* Item 099 $8.00 _____ _____

*contains reproducible masters

Shipping charges may be less if you call or e-mail your order, as books vary in weight. Slow mail is much cheaper.

Instructional Resources Company
3235 Garland
Wheat Ridge, CO 80033
                  or
Instructional Resources Company
P.O. Box 111704
Anchorage, AK 99511-1704
907-345-6689
Susan@SusanCAnthony.com
www.SusanCAnthony.com

Total _____

Shipping ($5.00 for first book,
   1.00 for each additional book) _____

Total enclosed _____

Enclose check or credit card number and expiration date.

Name _____

Organization _____

Address _____

_____

Phone number _____

❐ Teacher   ❐ Home School   ❐ Library   ❐ Other